ROBERT WALPOLE AND THE NATURE OF POLITICS IN EARLY EIGHTEENTH-CENTURY BRITAIN

British History in Perspective
General Editor: Jeremy Black

ROBERT WALPOLE AND THE NATURE OF POLITICS IN EARLY EIGHTEENTH-CENTURY BRITAIN

JEREMY BLACK

St. Martin's Press   New York

© Jeremy Black 1990

All rights reserved. For information, write:
Scholarly and Reference Division,
St. Martin's Press, Inc., 175 Fifth Avenue,
New York, N.Y. 10010

First published in the United States of America in 1990

Printed in Singapore

ISBN 0–312–04243–4

Library of Congress Cataloging-in-Publication Data
Black, Jeremy
Robert Walpole and politics in early eighteenth-century Britain
Jeremy Black.
     p.   cm.–(British history in perspectives)
   Includes bibliographical references.
   ISBN 0–312–04243–4
   1. Great Britain–Politics and government–1760–1789.   2. Great
Britain–Politics and government–1727–1760.   3. Great Britain–
–Social conditions–18th century.   4. Walpole, Robert, Earl of
Oxford, 1676–1745.   5. Pitt, William, Earl of Chatham, 1708–1778.
I. Title.   II. Series.
DA480.B58   1990
941.07'3–dc20
                                                    89-70081
                                                       CIP

CONTENTS

NOTE ON DATES

Unless otherwise stated all dates are given in old style, the British calendar of the period. Most European countries conformed to new style, which was eleven days ahead. New style dates are marked (ns).

PREFACE

There is not an evening, that there is not some paper cried about the street, good or bad of Robert hatch, Robert hangman, Robert the Coachman etc. or something of this kind, which shows what a spirit he has to fend himself against.

(Dowager Countess of Portland, 1730[1])

The most puzzling aspect of Sir Robert Walpole's political life is the extraordinary longevity of his ministry. Walpole was the leading minister of the Crown from 1721 until 1742 without a break. This contrasted with the periods before and after, which were characterised by ministerial instability. The longevity of Walpole's ministry is inextricably involved with the question of the stability of Britain in this period, and this notion of stability provides the key concept through which various aspects of Britain in this period can be discussed. Walpole's ministry raises the question whether a stability of ministerial personnel necessarily denoted an underlying stability in the economy, popular politics, religious feeling, constitutional concerns and national and regional relationships.

My work has greatly benefited from the studies of other scholars and from my own research. I am most grateful both for the former and to those bodies that have funded the latter, especially the British Academy. I would like to thank Stephen Baskerville, Ian Christie, Eveline Cruickshanks, Grayson Ditchfield, Richard Harding, Philip Woodfine and an anonymous reader for commenting on earlier versions and Linda Heitmann and Janet Forster for wordprocessing three of them. This book is dedicated to Jonathan Riley-Smith, my Director of Studies at Cambridge, and to Reg Ward, Professor of Modern History in my early years at Durham.

Newcastle, June 1989   J.B.

INTRODUCTION

Seventeenth-century background

To understand both Walpole and Britain in the first half of the
eighteenth century it is necessary to appreciate their seventeenth-
century background. This was the period when the leading
politicians were born and grew up. Of the leading Whigs,
Stanhope was born in 1673, Townshend and Sunderland in
1674, Walpole in 1676, Argyll in 1678, Ilay in 1682, Pulteney
in 1684 and Newcastle in 1693. Of the leading Tories, Strafford
was born in 1672, Shippen in 1673, Bolingbroke in 1678 and
Wyndham in 1687. These were years of serious instability and
conflict. The main interrelated causes were religious, political
and dynastic. Religious conflict was central to the great events
of the seventeenth century. The English Civil War can best be
appreciated, especially if its Scottish and Irish dimensions are
included, as a war of religion. James II (1685–8) was ousted in
the so-called Glorious Revolution largely because of the suspicion
that he would try to enforce his own Catholicism on his subjects.
Religious differences and suspicions corroded the loyalty and
obedience to the sovereign that so much contemporary political
thought preached. Religion was not only a matter for politicians.
People who were in the wrong Church were deprived of a wide
variety of what would today be considered rights but were then
thought of as privileges, such as the right to vote or to be an
MP, to hold political and government office, to establish schools

1

or to go to university. The anti-Catholic hysteria that accompanied the Popish Plot of 1678 and the violence that was directed against Dissenters (the growing denomination of Protestants who were not members of the Church of England) testified to the force of religious passion in the politics of the period and the extent to which it was by no means confined to those who wielded political power.

The overthrow of James had been prefigured in the Exclusion Crisis of 1679–81 when an attempt had been made to exclude him from the succession of his brother Charles II in favour of a Protestant heir, and again in the rebellion of Monmouth and Argyll in 1685. After his overthrow there were two claimants to the throne. The supporters of James and his descendants, known as Jacobites (from the Latin for James) were especially strong among the Catholics in Ireland and the Catholics and Episcopalians in Scotland. They also enjoyed a considerable measure of support in England, although its extent and determination is difficult to assess.

The throne itself was held by Protestants, first James's daughter Mary and her husband William III of Orange, then, because they had no children, by Mary's sister Anne and, after her death without issue in 1714, by the Lutheran Electors of Hanover, whose claim descended from the German marriage of James I's daughter. Their claim was recognised by Parliament in the Act of Settlement of 1701 but, in dynastic terms, they were clearly further from the Stuart line than James II's son, James, who claimed the throne from exile in France that year as 'James III' on the death of his father.

These conflicting claims led to invasion and conspiracies, suspicion and polemic that ranged from scurrilous verses to coherent ideological exchanges. Political disputes created and reflected political groups. The respective positions of Crown and Parliament were a matter of serious division. The political atmosphere of the period was one of hovering conflict and violence. Plots such as the Rye House Plot of 1683, a scheme to assassinate Charles II, were suppressed with violence. Judge Jeffreys tried and executed many of Monmouth's followers, only to end up dying in the Tower of London himself when the political climate changed. It was a time when an unsuccessful politician could expect parliamentary impeachment, exile, imprisonment and even execution. This was the political world in which Walpole grew up, and indeed Walpole himself was imprisoned in the Tower in 1712 by his Tory opponents.

Walpole's ministry did not banish instability. The Jacobite invasion of 1745 was ample evidence of the continued problem posed by dynastic conflict. It was only with the battle of Culloden in 1746, when Bonnie Prince Charlie, leading the army of Scottish Highlanders on behalf of his father, 'James III', was defeated by George II's younger son, the Duke of Cumberland, that the Hanoverian dynasty was really safe. However, Walpole's ministry did witness a lessening of political and religious tension that is readily apparent in comparison to the situation during the previous century. An evaluation of this change requires not only a consideration of his methods and policies, but also an examination of the nature of politics and government in the period, one that includes Scotland and Ireland as well as England and Wales.

1
WALPOLE'S RISE

The young Whig zealot

There was little about Walpole's political apprenticeship to
suggest that his ministry would be associated with stability, for
his first twenty years in politics were marked by wars, political
upheavals, and intense personal rivalries. Born in August 1676,
the son of a Norfolk country gentleman, Walpole was educated
at Eton and King's, Cambridge. A 'violent' Whig since at least
his Cambridge days, Walpole was extraordinarily ambitious. At
his first general election, that of 1701, he contested, without
success, one of the two Norfolk county seats, traditionally the
sphere of the well-connected and prestigious.

Elected in 1701 for Castle Rising, where his father had been
MP, and in 1702 for a more important Norfolk borough, the
port of King's Lynn, the seat he was thereafter to represent until
he was created Earl of Orford in February 1742, Walpole was
extremely active in the Whig cause in the House of Commons
in the 1700s, often speaking and acting as teller. Within three
months of his election in 1701, he was appointed to the
parliamentary committee to receive proposals for the payment
of the National Debt and for advancing the credit of the nation.

In his first session Walpole acted as a teller three times,
invariably on the Whig side. In the 1701–2 session Walpole was
a teller seven times including in February 1702 against an
amendment to prevent office-holders 'departing from the commu-

nion of the Church of England'. His six tellerships in the 1702–3 session included three on behalf of Whigs in contested elections, while in December 1702 Walpole moved unsuccessfully for leave to introduce a bill to resume all Crown grants made in James II's reign, a move which was aimed at the Tories who had then prospered. Elected to the leading Whig Club, the Kit-Kat, in 1703, in 1704 he was appointed to the Commons' committee to prepare the Address, soon to be a regular task, and was a teller against giving leave to bring in a bill against occasional conformity, the practice by which Dissenters avoided disqualification from office. In 1705 Walpole denied in the Commons Tory allegations that the Church was in danger, a stand on which he was consistent in these early years. He was also a gifted administrator and his abilities were rewarded. He was appointed to office as a member of the Admiralty Council 1705–8, Secretary at War 1708–10, and Treasurer of the Navy 1710–11 – all involved closely with the British war effort in the War of the Spanish Succession (1702–13). In 1708 Walpole sought to place army recruitment on a more orderly basis by introducing a system of county quotas but the proposal was rejected by the Commons. More prosaically, he was also concerned that year with delays in the supply of 'Biskett' for the forces.[1]

Walpole angered the Tories by his strident endorsement of Whig views, playing a major role in the attack on the Tory cleric Dr Sacheverell, who had argued that the Church was in danger under the Whig government. In December 1709, he spoke in support of the motion to declare Sacheverell's sermons 'seditious libels' and he was appointed to the committee to draw up the articles of his impeachment. His speech at the impeachment in February 1710 provides an unusual glimpse of Walpole in action, spelling out his Whig beliefs, justifying the resistance that had led to the overthrow of James II in 1688 and stressing the danger of high-church doctrines as laying the basis for arbitrary power,

> The doctrine of unlimited, unconditional passive Obedience, was first invented to support arbitrary & despotic power, & was never promoted or countenanced by any Government, that had not designs some time or other of making use of it. What then can be the design of preaching this doctrine now, unasked, unsought

for, in Her Majesty's reign, where the Law is the only Rule & measure of the Power of the Crown, & of the Obedience of the People? If then this doctrine can neither be an advantage or security to her Majesty, who neither wants or desires it, to what end or purpose must every thinking Man conclude it is now set on foot, but to unhinge the present Government, by setting aside all that has been done in opposition to that doctrine; & when by these means, the way is made clear to another title, the people are ready instructed to submit to whatever shall be imposed upon them. . . .

And all that the Doctor alledges in his Defence is, that in the Revolution there was no resistance at all; & that the King did utterly disclaim any such imputation. But surely, my Lords, it cannot be now necessary to prove Resistance in the Revolution; I should as well expect, that your Lordships would desire me for form's sake, to prove the Sun shines at Noon Day. If then, there was most undoubtedly Resistance used to bring about the Revolution, it will follow, that all the Censures, which are so freely bestowed upon Resistance in general, must attend, & will be imputed to the Revolution; & if *Resistance be utterly illegal, upon any pretence whatsoever*; if it is a *Sin*, which unrepented of, by the Doctrine of the Church of England, carries *sure & certain Damnation*; if, *upon repentance*, there is no *remission of Sins*, without a steadfast purpose to amend the Evil we have done, & to make all possible *Restitution*, or at least to do our utmost indeavour for that purpose; I beg your Lordships to consider what a duty is here professed, upon peril of damnation, upon every man's conscience, that knows, or believes, that there was resistance in the Revolution, and is conscious to himelf, of being in any ways assisting, or even consenting to this *damnable* sin; & what must be the consequence, if these doctrines, without any reserve or exception, are with Impunity preached throughout the Kingdom.[2]

The general election of 1710 saw a Tory landslide: when Walpole stood for the county of Norfolk he came bottom of the poll and was pelted by a Tory mob shouting 'no manager'. He was dismissed from office by the Tory ministry in 1711, nearly becoming involved in a duel with a Tory over a clash in the House. Walpole wrote pamphlets criticising the new ministry. His attack on the Tory attempt to negotiate peace in the winter of 1711–12 was interrupted by a successful Tory charge that he had received bribes whilst making the forage contracts for the army in Scotland in 1709–10. Voted guilty of 'a high breach of trust and notorious corruption', he was committed to the Tower of London and expelled from the House of Commons in January 1712. Walpole's imprisonment made him a national celebrity. Pamphlets, ballads and broadsheets were published for and against him, and in one Whig ballad he was described as 'the jewel in the Tower'. Returned for King's Lynn in the 1713 general election, he was one of the leaders of the Whig Opposition in the Commons in 1713–14, surviving attempts by the Tories to have him expelled again. He attacked the Schism Act, denying that the Dissenters were dangerous to Church and State, and argued that the Tory ministry threatened the Protestant Succession.

By the time of the accession of George I in 1714, Walpole had distinguished himself as one of the leading Whig parliamentarians. His rise had been rapid, and he was, by the standards of the day, a good party man. The Tory Jonathan Swift wrote of 'his bold, forward countenance, altogether a stranger to that infirmity which makes men bashful, joined to a readiness of speaking in public'.[3] An excellent parliamentary speaker, Walpole was a thoroughly political animal, adept at intrigue and at 'management', the handling of the patronage without which the political system and the administration could not operate. The Whig MP and journalist Richard Steele replied to the *Monitor*'s attack on Walpole as a libeller proficient in arrogance and deceit, by claiming that he had 'an open behaviour and honest countenance, a noble elocution, and many other qualities which render the gentleman the object of respect and love to all that know him . . . this gentleman is a perfect master in business, and has so clear a head, that he communicates his thoughts as perspicuously as they are placed in his own mind'. A pamphlet of 1716 referred to Walpole's vivacity, fine parts, deep judgement and penetration, another to his wisdom and 'golden tongue'. Not all comments were so favourable. A pamphleteer of 1711 termed him 'pragmatical, noisy and impertinent'.[4]

In Opposition, 1717–20

Given his political apprenticeship it might have been expected that Walpole would have sought after 1714 to put Whig schemes into practice. He did until 1717–20 when he led a group of Opposition Whigs who, in combination with the Tories, sought to thwart the government Whigs who were led by Stanhope and Sunderland. The latter were keen supporters of the system of intervention in European affairs associated with George I. They were also determined to reward the Dissenters, probably the most consistently loyal group of Whig supporters, by removing the legal bars that prevented them from holding office. George informed his first Privy Council that he wished for the repeal of the Occasional Conformity and Schism Acts passed under the Tory ministry in 1711 and 1714 respectively to curb the influence of the Dissenters.

The 'Whig Split' of 1717 arose essentially over the unwillingness of Walpole, who was by now First Lord of the Treasury and Chancellor of the Exchequer (1715–17), and his brother-in-law Lord Townshend, Secretary of State for the Northern Department (1714–16), to accept the foreign policy of George and Stanhope with its insistence on an active stance in Baltic politics. The Whig ministry was faced with a foreign ruler whose knowledge of British conditions was limited, but whose expectations, especially in the field of foreign policy, presented difficulties in terms of domestic politics. At the same time they had to cope with a rapidly changing international situation and were engaged in reversing many of the acts of the Tory ministry and in establishing Whig hegemony.

For most of the previous reign political debates on foreign policy had been subordinated to the needs of the war with France. A new situation emerged with the dual developments of an alliance with France, negotiated in 1716, and the accession of a Hanoverian ruler with German and Baltic interests of his own. This forced British politicians to define their attitudes towards states they knew little about, in the context of a rapidly changing international situation. Hanover's close involvement in the Great Northern War (1700–21) meant that George I expected from his British ministers a greater commitment to Hanoverian interests than he was subsequently to require or receive in the early 1720s. Differences of opinion over foreign policy were treated as tests of loyalty. Matters were made worse by the increasing favour shown by George to Stanhope and Sunderland from 1716, and by George's suspicions about the links between Townshend and Walpole and the Prince of Wales, a focus of opposition to the Court.

However, once he had gone into Opposition, Walpole, the leader of the Opposition Whigs in the Commons, was faced with the problem of creating a parliamentary group strong enough to show George I that he must accept Walpole and Townshend back into office. The only way to do so was to co-operate with the Tories, and this was what Walpole sought to do in 1717–20. In one parliamentary move in 1717 he was seconded by William Shippen, a Tory of pronounced Jacobite leanings 'who took the title of his good friend'. At the same time he was supported by George, Prince of Wales, then in dispute with his father.[5]

In 1720 George I found it expedient to settle his differences with his son and the ministry to settle theirs with Walpole. The parliamentary difficulties created by the Tory–Opposition Whig coalition played a role in this, as did the ministry's wish to ensure domestic support for their proposed confrontation with Russia over the latter's refusal to agree acceptable peace terms with Britain's new ally Sweden. Furthermore, both the ministry and the Opposition Whigs were united by 1720 in wishing to see the influence of Hanoverian ministers in British affairs limited.[6] In 1716–17 Stanhope and Sunderland had successfully used the Hanoverians against Walpole and Townshend, accusing the latter of failing to support Hanoverian interests. However, by 1719 Stanhope had changed his position and mounted a successful challenge to Bernstorff, the principal Hanoverian minister in London, over foreign policy.

On 24 April 1720 the Walpolean Whigs returned to Court, and in the following month Walpole steered a bill for paying the debts of the Civil List through the Commons, demonstrating his usefulness and his ability to handle fiscal topics. Later in his career, Walpole and his apologists sought to contrast his conduct in 1717–20 with the supposedly disloyal conduct of later oppositions. The ministerial London newspaper the *Daily Courant* claimed in 1734:

> he withdrew from Office without withdrawing from his Duty: He declined serving his late Majesty as a Minister, but persisted in the most submissive Obedience as a subject; he betrayed no private Conversations; he entered into no combinations; he aimed not at disturbing the Government, after he had quitted his share in it. Such a conduct failed not of obliging even those from whom he differed, and the concurring voice of all parties acknowledged his Virtue was without stain, and his Management without Reproach.[7]

These claims, made in response to Opposition criticisms of Walpole's inconsistency, were inaccurate, and reflected his unease when in office over his opposition to a Whig ministry in 1717–20. In fact his methods in 1717–20 were factious in the extreme and he did not hesitate to adopt every possible means to bring down the ministry. An Opposition pamphlet of 1731 suggested that Walpole had written a scandalous ballad during the Whig Split, adding 'that about that time he laid down his employments, and spurned as much against the Government (as his champions are pleased to call the Ministry) and distressed them as much in their measures as ever' Walpole's opponents had done since.[8] Spencer Compton, a political ally of Walpole in the late 1710s, secretly urged the Spanish envoy in London, Monteléon, to encourage Spain to resist British diplomatic moves, whilst Walpole was accused, with some reason, of hoping that the dispatch of a British fleet to the Mediterranean in 1718 to resist Spanish schemes would lead to difficulties.

In Parliament Walpole's oratory was violent. In April 1718 Charles Whitworth, the British envoy at The Hague, wrote: 'All the world here are extremely surprised at Mr. Walpole's conduct; they blame his impudence as well as his animosity'.[9] The Tories, whose support he sought, were bitterly opposed to the granting of further civil liberties to the Dissenters. Religious tension had not diminished with the accession of George I and it was fuelled by correct reports that the Dissenters, now more numerous than ever, perhaps 8 per cent of the population of England and Wales, wished to reverse the legislation that had been passed against them, in particular the Occasional Conformity and Schism Acts, and by rumours that they sought further rights. Uncertainty over ministerial views divided the higher echelons of the Church of England, so that the Whig split was not restricted to the laity. When motions for the repeal of the Occasional Conformity and Schism Acts were introduced in December 1718, Walpole joined the Tories in attacking the ministry's plans, comparing George I and Sunderland with James II and the latter's adviser, Sunderland's father. In December 1718, Lord Perceval reported:

> The Eldest Walpole gave offence to many by the free manner of his speaking. He told them he was turned out for not consenting to the repeal of these Bills; run parallels between King James and King George, declaring at the same time that although they were not justly drawn, the Jacobites would persuade the people they were; they have been told (said he) that King James recalled the Penal Laws and Tests, will they not be told King George recalls the security of the Church? they have been told King James set up a high commission court, will they not be told his present Majesty is now upon appointing commissioners for a Royal Visitation? ... then talking of the dissatisfactions of the People, and the disorders this Bill will probably produce in the Country, which he affirmed is against the judgement of even half of the Whigs, he said he had one comfort still and that was altho' His Majesty had been led into such ill measures they were not hereditary in the Royal Family for that he had a son who not only voted against the Bill but entered his protest ... he added that this consideration would keep the people quiet.[10]

The Duke of Montrose, who heard the speech, wrote, 'the most impertinent one I ever heard and I must own to you I am one of the very many that was surprised he was not taken up for it in an other manner than he was'. Walpole was criticised on the grounds that he had formerly opposed the Acts. An anonymous verse pamphlet of 1718 addressed to Walpole asked:

> Can the Fanatick schemes of Tories find
> Reception in your Penetrating Mind?
> Can such a Genius as yours believe
> The wild, and senseless Notions they receive?

But if, (as sure I think) you still disdain
The Visionary Systems, which they feign;
How can you join with them, and act a Part
Repugnant to the Dictates of your Heart?[11]

Tory–Opposition Whig co-operation, managed ably by Walpole, led the ministry to abandon the bulk of its legislative programme, which had been as markedly partisan as that of Queen Anne's Tory ministry of 1710–14. Aside from the ecclesiastical legislation, the other major element had been the Peerage Bill, defeated in 1719. This had been an attempt to restrict the membership of the House of Lords, and thus to prevent the future George II from creating fresh peers when he came to the throne in order to buttress a new Walpole ministry which he might appoint. Legislation to increase government control over the English universities, the training centres of the Anglican clergy, was dropped because of the strength of likely opposition.[12]

Walpole and the Tories

Stanhope and Sunderland did not live to be disgraced by the future George II. Their deaths, in 1721 and 1722 respectively, helped Walpole to consolidate his newly-restored position in the ministry and among the Whigs. He was determined to control both and his success in so doing was crucial to his continuance in office.

Unlike Robert Harley, the leading Tory minister in 1710–14, Walpole condemned the idea of a mixed ministry. When in 1723 Bolingbroke proposed one to him, Walpole 'answered it was both impossible and unadvisable for me to enter into any such negotiation'. That summer Townshend wrote to Walpole about another approach for a mixed ministry: 'I think the manner in which you received Lord Kinnoull's overtures was exactly right, since nothing can be more dangerous than to enter into negotiations with the Tories, or even to labour under the suspicion of it at this time.'[13] Walpole argued that the Tories were sympathetic to the Jacobite cause, that of the Stuart

Pretender, 'James III'. In February 1716 he attacked the Tories in the House of Commons:

> Walpole . . . set forth the carriage of one set of men among us, who tho' ty'd by the strongest obligations of religion as well as by their interest and their country's welfare to support the King against the Pretender, had yet in all their conversation and behaviour affected to express an indifference for the success of the rebellion which sort of men (he said) differed from declared rebels only in that they wanted courage to draw the sword.[14]

This remained Walpole's attitude throughout his ministry. He was convinced that Jacobitism was a serious threat and that the Tories were willing to support the Jacobite cause. The extent to which this was true has been debated by historians without any generally accepted conclusion being reached. It has recently been argued that Jacobitism was a popular force after 1715.[15] What is clear is that there was considerable anxiety about Jacobitism and that this was of political importance. Walpole established a most efficient network to spy on the Jacobites and was aware that they could become a very serious threat, given sufficient foreign assistance.[16] The assumption that politics was essentially a struggle between Jacobites and supporters of the Protestant Succession was not held by Walpole alone. Indeed it was a powerful basis of Whig loyalty that helped to tarnish Opposition Whigs, such as Walpole in the late 1710s. In 1719 Newcastle had written to Stanhope, 'the great point I think we ought to aim at is, that there should be but two parties that for and that against the Government and I cannot but think that by a new election, Mr. Walpole and the few friends his party will be able to bring in, will be so incorporated with the Jacobites, that we shall have but little difficulty in dealing with them'.[17]

Though determined to prevent the Tories from gaining power, Walpole when in office followed policies that did not challenge Tory views excessively. Walpole's policies contrasted with the alarmist Tory propaganda concerning Whig intentions that had been produced from 1714 onwards. There was no comparison between Walpole's policies and those attributed to the Whigs in such Tory tracts as Francis Atterbury's *English Advice to the*

Freeholders of England (1715). His foreign policy, with its stress on minimising foreign commitments and thus ending the need for subsidy treaties with foreign states and enabling the ministry to reduce taxation, corresponded with traditional Tory notions. In 1723 Walpole responded to an apparent Baltic crisis by writing 'my Politics are to keep free from all engagements as long as we possibly can'. He also expressed the fear that a competition among the ministers to win George I's favour by supporting his diplomatic projects would lead Britain 'into very rash engagements'.[18] The French envoy in London, Chavigny, noted in 1734 that Walpole and the opposition shared common views on foreign policy. Two years later he reported a conversation with Walpole in which the latter expressed delight that he was free of the bad system that Stanhope had left him with and that Britain was no longer closely involved in European affairs. These were views that the Tories could accept. In 1718 the ministerial MP, Sir David Dalrymple, claimed that the Opposition through their 'enmity to the Government have wrought up this nation to a hatred of war though unavoidable and the country gentlemen . . . cry out against taxes'.

That year, when in Opposition, Walpole had joined with the Tories in attacking both the Quadruple Alliance, by which Britain had become closely involved in Italian politics, and the dispatch of a fleet to the Mediterranean to protect the Austrian position in Italy against Spanish attack. In 1732, 1733 and 1734, when the Austrians pressed the Walpole ministry to send a fleet to prevent a similar attack, no ships were sent. Similarly the Walpole ministry resisted pressure to become involved first in the contested election of 1733 for the throne of Poland and then in the subsequent War of the Polish Succession of 1733–5. In this respect Walpole's stance corresponded more closely with that of the Tories than it did either with some of his ministerial colleagues or with the group of Opposition Whigs led by William Pulteney, both of which sought intervention in the war on the Austrian side. War was seen by Walpole as a threat to the political order.[19]

Walpole's religious policy

The Tory party tended to see itself as the defender of the Anglican Church, threatened by the Dissenters and their political allies the Whigs. The strength of religious feeling and the continued vitality of religious divisions in early eighteenth-century Europe must not be underestimated, and Britain, as in so much else, was no exception to the usual European situation. Religious divisions played a major role in late seventeenth-century politics and had been largely responsible for the bitterness of the party struggle between the Whigs and Tories.[20] Walpole's refusal to legislate in favour of the Dissenters played a major role in reducing the political consequences of religious differences. In 1718, when in Opposition, he spoke vigorously in defence of the position of the Church of England and this became his policy when in office. Walpole pointed out to Tories, such as Edward Harley, that he took 'care of the Church'.[21] After 1719 the Whigs dropped Church matters from their legislative programme.

The political difficulties that arose in 1736 when Church issues were again widely debated in Parliament confirmed the wisdom of the policy for the intervening years.[22] Walpole preferred to manage the Church and universities by means of patronage rather than by legislation and administrative innovation. Filling vacant bishoprics was a more congenial form of management, and the staunchly Anglican Whig Lord Perceval was able to write in 1722: 'When a few more of the Dignitaries drop off and a little care shall be taken of the Universities, we may hope to see a thorough change in the clergy, and then they will recover the esteem which they have forfeited through the misbehaviour of too many yet remaining among them.' Five years later a Jacobite complained that the ministry had the support of all the bishops that attended Parliament.[23]

The cry of 'the Church in danger' was heard less frequently in the 1720s and early 1730s, when an effective co-operation between Walpole and the most influential cleric, Bishop Gibson of London, replaced the tension between the Stanhope–Sunderland ministry and Archbishop Wake. In 1751 a Dissenter wrote: 'the generality of the Bench have learnt of Sir Robert Walpole . . .

15

to regard and insist on the Act of Toleration as the Boundary between the Established Church, and the Dissenters: . . . no favour is to be expected either from the Government or their Lordships beyond what that Act by a fair construction entitles us to.'[24]

Walpole's ecclesiastical policy helped to lessen political tension, though the Tories remained concerned over the position of the Dissenters, and there was no reintroduction of the Occasional Conformity Act. Furthermore, the Whig monopoly of higher clerical positions and the promotion of clerics judged heterodox by the Tories aroused fury. Bishop Hoadly, a low-churchman long dreaded by the high-Church faction as intending to level all barriers between the Church and Dissent, had his party zeal rewarded successively with the bishoprics of Bangor (1715), Hereford (1721), Salisbury (1723) and Winchester (1734). Walpole did not strike commentators as especially religious and his attitude offended many. Dr Wilkes, a Staffordshire doctor, noted in his diary: 'There never was . . . in this nation a set of men who laughed so much at religion . . . as Sir Robert Walpole and his hirelings have done'. Walpole's faith was certainly not intellectual. His son Horace recorded in 1750 that the new Bishop of Durham was 'a metaphysical author, much patronised by the late Queen: she never could make my father read his book . . . he told her, his religion was fixed, and that he did not want to change or improve it.'[25] The role of political, especially parliamentary, rather than religious, considerations in church appointments can be seen in a letter written in 1743 by Newcastle to Carteret, then with George II in the Empire (Germany). Newcastle was Recorder of Nottingham:

> I am again to trouble your Lordship with relation to a living which is vacant, and in His Majesty's gift. I mean the Vicarage of Claybrooke in Leicestershire. I send your Lordship inclosed an application from the Mayor and Aldermen of Nottingham on behalf of Mr. Hutchinson, a gentleman of one of the first families in that county, and whose brother has an estate there of upwards of £2,000 a year. The Gentleman himself is extremely well qualified in every respect, and most zealous for His Majesty's interest. I humbly hope His Majesty will be so good, as to confer this living

upon him; and that the more, as the town of Nottingham, and the City of Bristol were the only towns in all England, that sent up contrary Instructions to their Members, and this present mark of favour to the Corporation of Nottingham will be extremely well received, and may soon have a good effect: Mr. Warren, one of their present members, and a very violent Tory, is so ill, that it is thought he cannot last many weeks: and I am persuaded, that, in case of his death, we shall have a very zealous, and a very good Whig chosen in his room.[26]

In the late 1730s renewed pressure from the Dissenters, and the breakdown of the alliance with Gibson, due to a clash over religious patronage and differences over the tithe question, created difficulties. However, there was no resumption of the Stanhope–Sunderland programme of repeal and Walpole took care not to support the Dissenters excessively, with the one important exception of the Tithe Bill of 1736, to which he underestimated the likely opposition. Walpole was genuinely shaken by the clergy's attack (unforgivably, in his view, supported and articulated by Gibson), the one time he almost forgot the lesson of Sacheverell and provoked clergy-led popular Toryism. However, Walpole was unwilling to support repeal of the Test and Corporation Acts. His policy in the crisis of 1718 prefigured his subsequent policy. The ministry's decision in 1718–19 to drop the proposed legislation in favour of the Dissenters, particularly that pertaining to the corporations, removed a substantial challenge to the control of the Tory gentry over much of provincial England. Such a challenge, reminiscent in some ways of late Stuart policies (Walpole in 1718 compared government schemes with those of James II, who had created alarm by his pro-Dissenter policy), was not to be repeated. The merest suggestion that the envisaged extension of the Excise legislation in 1733 would lead to the imposition of a new level of central government control provoked strong opposition. The largely undisturbed government of Britain's localities in the age of Walpole was one of the most characteristic features of the period. It was also part of the unstated relationship between Walpole and the political community that helped to produce, and was itself the product of, stability.

Taxation

The Excise proposals of 1733, withdrawn in response to a storm of parliamentary and press criticism, were part of a fiscal strategy that reflected Walpole's desire to woo rural political opinion, much of which was Tory. He hoped to transfer the bulk of taxation from land – the land tax – to consumption. From 1722 to 1726, in 1730, and again from 1733–9, Walpole was able to keep the land tax down to two shillings (ten pence in today's money) in the pound, and in 1731 and 1732 he managed to cut it to one shilling. When the rate rose in 1727 in order to finance the military expenditure created by a cold war with Austria and Spain, a Jacobite observed 'the four shillings in the pound does affect the landed men'.[27] Since the assessments for the land tax were largely traditional ones, not reflecting the current value of property, low rates of taxation were a double concession to the landed groups – that is, the politically vital groups – in society. This policy was helped by peace and by Walpole's astute handling of the National Debt, but it depended on an ability to raise indirect taxation. In 1732 Walpole reintroduced the salt duty which he had abolished two years earlier. He argued that it was a fair tax as nearly everyone contributed to it: the Opposition speakers retorted that the poor had to spend a larger proportion of their income to pay the duty. The following year he proposed to extend the Excise to wine and tobacco. His failure to do so reflected the Opposition's success in exploiting largely misplaced fears concerning the intention and consequences of the scheme, though Excise was always unpopular. Walpole himself regarded the scheme as simply another technical financial measure similar to many that were passed regularly by the ministry. He was confident that Parliament would support the scheme and was unable to understand the public outcry that it aroused.[28]

Walpole and the localities

The willingness of the ministry to allow local landowners to rule their localities contrasted with developments in certain other states in Europe. Although it is now widely accepted that 'absolutism' is a misnomer when used to describe European states in the period 1650–1750 and that the governments of these states did not seek to destroy aristocratic power, it is nevertheless true that some states, particularly Prussia, Russia and Sardinia, and in the later eighteenth century, Austria, witnessed serious attempts to extend central control of the localities, partly by means of enrolling the aristocracy in the service of the state. In late seventeenth-century Britain there had been intimations of a similar policy.

However, the eighteenth century witnessed an extraordinary divergence between on the one hand the remarkable growth and increased sophistication of central government agencies, particularly the navy, the state fiscal system (the most sophisticated in Europe) and the Excise,[29] and on the other the manner in which the localities were governed. Essentially this was a matter of self-government by the propertied. The ministry relied upon Justices of the Peace, who were usually prominent local landowners. The Land Tax Commissioners were also local gentry and the tax was notorious for the unfairness of its assessments, with wide disparities between particular counties. Thus Britain, which in the Bank of England and the Treasury had two of the most sophisticated institutions in monarchical Europe, also had a direct tax system that was operated in an inefficient and unfair fashion. There was no attempt in Britain to introduce a land survey that could serve as a rational basis for taxation, as happened in Lombardy and Piedmont.[30]

The Whigs carried out a purge of many of the Tory JPs after they came to power in 1714, and judging from Lancashire and Cheshire it was most marked in 1716. This purge had achieved its aim by 1719, ensuring that the Tories had only minority status in the Commissions of the Peace, and Walpole made no effort to complete it. It sufficed that the Tories were not strong enough to dominate the Commissions; there was no attempt to remove them completely from positions of authority. There was, therefore, a difference in character between the proscription of the Tories in the 1710s and that under Walpole. Whether the

Stanhope–Sunderland ministry would have sought to extend their assault on the legal position of the Church of England and their attempt to remodel the House of Lords (the Peerage Bill) and the universities by attempting to alter the nature of local government in Britain is unclear. The purge of other local offices (Lord Lieutenancy, Deputy Lieutenancies, Custos Rotulorum, Duchy offices in Cornwall and Lancaster) was more complete than that of the JPs. Only the shrievalty, which was a financial burden, was left to Tories. It could be suggested that the remodelling of borough charters in order to alter local government and parliamentary representation was not practical politics for any party after 1688 because the entire political class was affected by the legacy of James II and caught up in its propaganda on this point. However, this would probably not have dissuaded Sunderland. What is clear is that Walpole had no such intentions. Purging the JPs to ensure that the existing system operated in favour of the ministry was not the same as seeking to change the fundamental nature of that system. However, many of the new Whig JPs were not of gentry origins, and this was greeted with outrage in what was still an extremely hierarchical society in which social status was held to equate with merit. The Tories pressed for higher landed qualifications for JPs in 1719 and 1722, succeeded in 1732, and tried to take it further in 1745 and 1747.[31] Walpole's policy was to avoid provoking the Tories, but this did not mean that they were satisfied. Their opposition was contained, not conciliated. They remained proscribed, and careers in some of the professions, so valuable for the younger sons of the landed gentry, were effectively closed to the Tories. The armed forces had been purged in 1714–15, and few Tories were appointed thereafter. A new Commission for Army Debts was established in 1715 to replace the Tory one. Promotion to senior positions in the Church, the law, the diplomatic service and at Court was far easier for Whigs, and many of the Tories appointed owed their positions to willingness to avoid political commitments. The cut in the land tax benefited Whig country gentlemen as well as Tories.

The Whigs purged the JPs, not because they hoped to carry out a revolution in government, but because they were unsure of the loyalties of the Tories and anxious about the security situation. The purge can be seen as a response to the Jacobite rising in 1715 rather than as the first stage in an attempt to create a Whig absolutism. It would be wrong to ascribe to Walpole alone Britain's failure to follow the continental trend and to become an absolutism, an enlightened despotism or a well-ordered police state, terms that have been used to describe European developments. The situation was far more complex, and, in particular, it is necessary to consider the legacy of late seventeenth-century developments – the Glorious Revolution of 1688, and the limitations on monarchical power devised subsequently in 1689–1701 – and the political culture of Britain, a society where resistance and contractual theories were of great importance, particularly as a result of recent history. However, it is true that under the first two Georges opportunities existed for increasing government authority. The suppression of the Jacobite rising of 1715 helped to discredit the Opposition, just as the failures of the Rye House Plot (1683) and of the Argyll and Monmouth risings (1685) helped to strengthen the position of Charles II and James II. James was overthrown by a foreign invasion, while, in contrast, in the 1720s and 1730s the Jacobite position was actually undermined by a peaceful foreign policy offering little prospect of support for a pro-Stuart invasion. Britain was in alliance with France, its most dangerous potential rival, from 1716 until the Anglo-Austrian alliance of 1731, the Second Treaty of Vienna. Walpole's foreign policy ensured that conflict was avoided with France for the rest of the decade. Walpole's systematic use of the resources of ministerial patronage helped to keep Parliament quiescent. The ministry regularly enjoyed large majorities, and Opposition campaigns to bring about its fall were singularly unsuccessful. In 1731–2 the *Parlement* of Paris, the leading judicial body in France, created more problems than did the Westminster Parliament for their respective ministries.

A minister like Sunderland might have sought to exploit this situation in order to increase government power in Britain, or to make opposition more difficult. There could have been a systematic remodelling of borough charters or a reimposition of press censorship. The latter was certainly mentioned on several occasions. That no such steps were taken was partly due to Walpole. He helped to block Sunderland's schemes in the late 1710s by creating a powerful Opposition. Lord Bolingbroke and William Pulteney sought to create in the late 1720s and 1730s a 'country' opposition that would unite Tories and Opposition Whigs.[32] Their attempt failed to bring down Walpole. Instead it was he who was most successful in fusing elements of the Whig and Tory inheritance. The 1710s had seen extreme, partisan government, first by the Tories, and then by the Whig Stanhope–Sunderland ministry. One commentator observed in 1715, 'when great employments are given to great men, it is natural for them to wish their friends, relations and dependents should be under them in the inferior offices rather than strangers and friends to a late ministry'.[33] Walpole benefited from a disenchantment with this experience, a growing conservatism in Whig thought[34] and the end of the War of the Spanish Succession and its attendant political tensions. His ministry was very much a Whig one in its composition, but the policies he followed, particularly in ecclesiastical affairs, and the initiatives he deliberately refrained from taking helped to ensure widespread acquiescence in the continuance of the ministry. Unlike during the Stanhope–Sunderland ministry, ministerial Whiggery absorbed enough of moderate Toryism under Walpole to make itself generally acceptable to a fundamentally conservative nation.

2

STABILITY, PATRONAGE AND PARLIAMENT

Stability

Walpole's success raises the general issue of British stability in a period when there was a considerable degree of dissent and occasional unrest. Plumb has drawn attention to the political changes that helped to create a context for stability, such as the passage of the Septennial Act of 1716 under which it was necessary to have a general election only every seven years. The Earl of Stair reported from Paris that, 'the passing of this bill for changing the duration of Parliaments gives credit to the King's affairs here and makes them consider the ministry as better established and less precarious'. The Whigs claimed that the previous system, by which, under the Triennial Act of 1694, elections had to be held at least every three years, had led to disorderly elections and the bankruptcy of candidates by frequent expenses. The increasing cost of contesting definitely discouraged some candidates from standing and it appears to have encouraged electoral pacts by which the Whigs and Tories divided the representation to English boroughs and counties, each of which returned two MPs, with the exception of London and Weymouth and Melcombe Regis, each of which returned four. The representation of Knaresborough was divided between local Whig and Tory interests and the constituency was not contested after the 1715 general election until 1784.

Holmes has argued that demographic stagnation and social

changes, such as the creation of professional jobs that could help to reduce unemployment among the younger sons of the gentry, helped to create the social stability, without which political stability was not possible. He has also drawn attention to the demographic and economic conditions that helped to ensure that popular radicalism was limited. Holmes argued that the bulk of the gentry, even when excluded from national power, held back from whipping up popular support against the political system, and were in any case mollified by relative economic prosperity. The same prosperity meant that neither the lower nor the 'middling' orders had grievances serious enough to provoke them into radical political action.[1]

Other historians have questioned the degree of stability. Kenyon has drawn attention to the violence of public life, and to the weakness of the ministry in the face of public pressure. Colley has argued that the proscription of the Tories endangered 'class unity' and produced 'an unprecedented rift in the landed elite – the vital pre-condition of real political instability'.[2] Those scholars who have stressed the importance of Jacobitism have reminded us of a powerful challenge to the Hanoverian system. Cruickshanks has drawn a distinction between parliamentary stability which she argues reflects 'the inability of the Tories to mount an effective and sustained opposition campaign', and the absence of the corresponding political stability outside Parliament.[3] The latter is particularly clear when attention is directed to Jacobitism, Scotland and Ireland. Other scholars have drawn attention to evidence of popular radicalism and resistance to the policies of the Whig oligarchy.[4]

Clearly an assessment of Walpole's skill in maintaining domestic peace is related to the vexed question of stability. The disorders of the 1740s – the ministerial weakness that led to the fall of Walpole in 1742, the Jacobite rising in 1745, and ministerial divisions and conflict with the king – would suggest that it is important not to exaggerate the political stability of the period. Under the stress of war the Walpolean system proved less resilient than it had done hitherto. Equally, the absence of serious radical political pressure from the lower and middling orders in the 1740s when the political nation was divided and vulnerable suggests that it would be wrong to regard the preceding Walpolean period as one in which radicalism was suppressed by force or the threat of force. Indeed had there been such a challenge from below in the 1740s it is doubtful whether the non-Jacobite elite could have afforded the luxury of such strong disagreement within itself.

At times troops were used by Walpole to restore order, particularly in labour disputes when workers had resorted to sometimes quite dramatic violence, such as pulling down houses and mills. The Wiltshire clothworkers of Trowbridge were one group who suffered as a result. The government could use capital punishment to restore order, one Under-Secretary writing in 1723: ' 'Tis certain the Salisbury Court execution put an end to a great deal of foolish and dangerous rioting; if the Frogs are grown so familiar with the Log, as the fable has it, as to jump upon it again, power must be exerted to let them know their King, and the Law that should keep them in awe.'[5] However, continental commentators, such as the Comte de Cambis, French ambassador 1737–40, were amazed at the extent to which popular disturbances in Britain were not punished and law and order were flouted. Given the limited resources for coercion at the disposal of the ministry – there were fewer than 15,000 troops stationed in England – it would have been difficult to suppress widespread popular disturbances. However, it was not necessary to do so. Many riots were very specific in their aims, often seeking to fix the price of bread in times of dearth at a level judged acceptable in the popular 'moral economy'. Social inequality was accepted by the bulk of the population, and general attitudes were far more conservative and placid or apathetic than any concentration on urban radicalism might suggest. British society was predominantly rural; the percentage of the population of England and Wales living in towns of 2500 inhabitants or more was 18.7 in 1700 and 22.6 in 1750 (see Wrigley and Schofield, 1981). Until the 1790s there was no need for a coalition of the property-owning classes to defend property and order, if only because the mass of the people saw no way of displacing the existing structures, and even in the 1790s the coalition was far from complete.

The Walpole ministry was not, therefore, placed uneasily upon a seething mass of popular resentment. There were violent popular disturbances, such as those in London in protest against the Gin Act of 1736, an act that had more effect on the city population than most legislation. However, there were fewer popular disturbances directed against the ministry in England in the 1720s and 1730s than there had been in the 1710s and violence or the threat of violence played less part in politics than in the late seventeenth century.

Furthermore, attitudes to violence are not constant. British society in the eighteenth century was more accustomed to violence than in the 1960s and 1970s and it is important not to use the violence of the period as an indicator of instability. Writing in 1977, Kenyon took the mobbing of Walpole during the Excise agitation as a sign of instability.[6] A historian writing twelve years later might not regard it as so remarkable.

Walpole as financial manager

Finance represented one of the greatest sources of difficulties for eighteenth-century European governments. By European standards Britain was, for a major power, in a singularly fortunate position. The funded National Debt based on the Bank of England, founded in 1694, enabled British ministries to borrow large sums at low rates of interest. Whereas in the early 1690s the government was paying up to 14 per cent for long-term loans, the rate of interest fell to 6–7 per cent in 1702–14, 4 per cent in the late 1720s, at or below 3 per cent in the late 1730s, and after a wartime rise, to 3 per cent in 1750. The system was not, however, without its problems, both political and financial. There was considerable concern about the rise in the National Debt. Due essentially to war expenditure this rose significantly. Over 30 per cent of the total government expenditure during the Nine Years War and the War of the Spanish Succession was financed by public borrowing and the National Debt at George I's accession was £40 million, with an annual interest charge of £2 million. The size of the debt worried contemporaries who feared not only the drain of annual interest payments to creditors, but also the possibility of national bankruptcy. Its very size might discourage further loans, or in the event of a crisis of confidence, cause a run on the Bank as creditors sought the return of their capital. When Walpole became First Lord of the Treasury for the first time in October 1715 the bulk of the redeemable National Debt still carried interest at over 6 per cent. After studying the whole area of finance, Walpole was responsible for a plan put forward by the Commons, sitting as a Committee of the Whole House in March 1717. This envisaged a number of changes, including reducing the interest on the redeemable part of the debt to 5 per cent and repaying dissentients. The savings made by the reduction of the interest were to be paid into a Sinking Fund, to be used to help repay the debt. Although Walpole resigned in April, the Stanhope–Sunderland ministry had most of the proposals enacted that summer. By the late 1720s the Sinking Fund had increased to over £1 million a year. Thanks to this Walpole was able to cut the debt by nearly £13 million by his fall in 1742 but, because he increased the debt by £$6\frac{1}{2}$ million worth of new borrowing, the net decrease was only £$6\frac{1}{4}$ million. This was only a small part of the debt but, due to further reductions in interest payments, Walpole was able to make a bigger percentage cut in the annual charge of the debt. This fell from over £2 million in 1721 to £1,890,000 in 1741. Such measures increased confidence and in turn made it easier to conduct the government's financial affairs at a reasonable rate of interest. The beneficial political consequences that were anticipated from financial restructuring and restraint were outlined in the *Supplement to the Freeholder's Journal* of 14 December 1722. The anonymous article made it clear that such consequences should influence parliamentary conduct. Thus, Walpole's influence in the Commons was designed to foster a financial regime of economy and debt reduction while his success in introducing this regime was held up as a reason for the maintenance of his influence:

> The confining the expence of the year 1723 to the usual malt tax and two shillings in the pound on land, the raising of this

supply at an interest not exceeding 3 per cent and the reducing of above one million of the short annuities from 5 to 3% interest . . . must be a very agreeable surprise to all the freeholders of Great Britain, and give them the pleasing hopes, that the National Debt will, for the future, annually decrease; and that the taxes, which are most grievous to the People, and especially those which are discouraging to our trade and manufactures, will gradually lessen. This undoubtedly will, and perhaps nothing else can, effectually support the National Credit; and will also greatly tend to cure those discontents and dissatisfactions which are apprehended to be very general . . . it seems to be the indispensable duty of every gentleman in the House of Commons . . . to contribute their utmost assistance to the effecting so good a work.

However, the use to which the Sinking Fund was put was not free from criticism. It was regarded as insufficient on the basis of the failure to pay off most of the debt. This peacetime failure, repeated during subsequent periods of peace, ensured that after each war the debt was at a new high. It rose appreciably during the conflicts of 1739–48 and 1756–63 and in 1775, on the eve of another major war, it stood at £127 million. An anonymous writer, who in 1813 praised the introduction of income tax as an attempt to equalise revenue and expenditure, claimed that:

From the period of the complete introduction of the Funding System . . . to the close of the American War, the object of our measures of finance during war appeared to be only to provide for the immediate expenses of the year, by borrowing such sums as were necessary for any extraordinary charge incurred, and by imposing such taxes as might meet the interest of the loan leaving to the period of peace the consideration of any provision for the repayment of debt; and this being attempted at irregular periods and on no permanent system, was never carried into effectual execution; the total amount of debt redeemed between the Peace of Utrecht and the close of the American war being no more than £8,330,000.[7]

Part of the reason for this was Walpole's use of the Sinking Fund for other purposes. The fund had no trustees appointed to regulate it and ministers, following Walpole's example, were to be tempted to use it, with parliamentary consent, to alleviate difficulties.

The Sinking Fund was used by Walpole as security for new loans, to anticipate annual taxes, and to meet specific problems. In 1727 the extra £100,000 Walpole needed to increase George II's Civil List to £800,000 came from the fund and in 1733–4 the fall in revenues produced by the cut of the land tax to 1 shilling in the pound, and the need to arm in response to the prospect of intervention in the War of the Polish Succession, was met by drawing from the fund, a policy that was to be followed thereafter by Walpole. In effect the land tax was kept low, with beneficial political consequences, by delaying the repayment of the National Debt. This use of the Sinking Fund aroused considerable criticism and was taken by Opposition spokesmen to be further evidence of an undesirable level of financial manipulation on the part of Walpole. Had more of the debt been redeemed then the annual interest charge, which had to be met through taxation or new loans, would have fallen correspondingly. The hope that this annual charge could be cut was one of the reasons for the 1737 proposal from Sir John Barnard, MP for the City of London, that interest rates on government debts should be cut from 4 to 3 per cent. John Drummond MP expressed the hope that the cut would allow the government to 'take off the soap and candle and leather taxes or what should be found most burdensome to the people and manufacturers'. The measure divided politicians along unfamiliar lines but Walpole helped to defeat it on the grounds that it would harm small investors, limit ministerial flexibility in financial policy and be difficult to implement. The defeat also protected the interest enjoyed by the major city financiers whom Walpole was close to and who were vital lenders to the government.[8] It was to help them that Walpole had defeated an attempt in 1730 by Barnard to end the East India Company's monopoly of trade with India and the Far East.

The details of financial policy were contentious, as the Excise crisis of 1733 and the reduction of interest controversy in 1737 made clear. However, the general thrust of Walpole's financial policy was popular. Walpole wanted to keep taxes low, particularly taxes on an agricultural interest affected by stagnation, and he felt that the maintenance of peace was the best means to achieve this. He sought successfully to bring order and stability to government finances both because he believed that that would make it easier to finance government and because he argued that such stability was essential to the rest of the economy. His success arose from his ability, not least his comprehensive understanding of the interrelated complexities of public finance, his connections and his strong sense of practicality. The numerous financial memoranda in his surviving papers testify to his energy in this field. Dedication to public finance was accompanied on Walpole's part by measures to aid economic activity. He attempted to develop British industry and trade. In 1722 the export duties on most British manufactured products were abolished. Import duties on foreign raw materials required for these products were reduced or abolished. Potential competitors within the British empire, in Ireland and North America, were hindered. Attempts were made to improve the customs service. Walpole was not alone among politicians in his interest in economic and financial affairs but he displayed an impressive aptitude and consistency of purpose. His high reputation as a financial manager was well deserved even though his role as a minister concerned with money helped to encourage criticism of him on the grounds both of supposed personal corruption and of the use of corrupt practices in order to entice others to provide support.

Corruption

A phobia about corruption inspired much of the political and literary criticism of Walpole's ministry. Most of the leading literary figures of the period – including Pope, Swift, Gay and Johnson – attacked Walpole, alleging that he governed through corruption and that his attitudes were debasing British public life and society. These arguments were advanced also in one of the most interesting newspapers of the period, the *Craftsman*, a London weekly produced by Bolingbroke and Pulteney. In the issue of 25 May 1728 the paper stated that 'what are commonly called great abilities, in this age, will appear, upon enquiry, to be nothing but a little sordid genius for tricks and cunning, which founds all its success on corruption, stockjobbing and other iniquitous arts'. *The Knight and the Prelate*, a ballad of 1734, proclaimed:

> In the Island of Britain I sing of a K....t,
> Much fam'd for dispensing his favour aright,
> No Merit could he but what's palpable see,
> And he judg'd of Men's Worth by the Weight of their Fee.

The strength of the literary opposition to Walpole has impressed posterity, but it reflected rather his neglect of the literati of the age than any particular faults of his administration. As John Andrews wrote in 1785: 'Sir Robert Walpole, by neglecting men of letters, drew the whole load of their odium upon him. Hence it is, that no mercy hath been shown to his character; and that he is, according to the representations of the majority of writers accounted the chief author and modeller of that regular system of corruption which has nearly subverted the constitution.'[9]

This reputation stuck, though Dr Johnson in his later years thought much more favourably of Walpole. The *Gazetteer* of 3 July 1770 referred to Walpole as 'that patron of venality'. In 1786 the *Universal Daily Register*, a London newspaper, reported, without any evidence, that:

> Sir Robert Walpole, who had been for many years the minister of Great Britain, and who brought the system of venality and corruption to a more alarming excess than had ever been known previous to his time . . . shamefully declared that to make the people quiet and submissive to his measures, he found it his best policy to keep them poor, and work upon what he facetiously called the consumptive plan. – He publicly argued in support of that corruption which he had practised secretly; and indeed too many of later date have not blushed openly to adopt his principles.

When, in 1768, Philip Thicknesse wrote in praise of Walpole he was conscious that this was an unusual position. 'I own I am such an enemy to my country, as to wish Sir Robert Walpole among us again; he was a staunch Whig, not absolutely destitute of abilities, and what money he idled away, was among his friends at home; not in fruitless fantastical expeditions on the coast of France',[10] the last comment being an attack on Pitt's strategy during the Seven Years War (1756–63). This contrasting of Walpole and Pitt was interesting because in general the contrast, which was made both during the eighteenth century and subsequently, was to the disadvantage of Walpole who was criticised for pusillanimity in the face of France and Spain and for corruption. Walpole did not play to the gallery, did not appeal to the wider political nation, to the extent that Pitt was to do, and his reputation suffered as a result. Walpole's ministry was not as glorious as that of Pitt, when much of the British empire was acquired.

In 1758 a leading London opposition journal invited its readers to:

> look back to the administration of Sir Robert Walpole: Did not the Chancellor of the Exchequer, that he might be allowed to govern without jealousy, connive at every abuse of power, and every breach of trust in those, who had it in their power to thwart his measures? Did not his measures expose the dignity of his master to contempt? and his country to shame and disgrace? for which he suffered the fate of a bad minister: the people cried for justice, and the wrath of the king went out against him: he was disgraced.
>
> Under such an administration the council become a cabal; where a few private men, without the least regard or esteem for one another, mutually combine to support the share they have usurped amongst themselves in the government of the kingdom.

Walpole was referred to as 'that Grand Corruptor' or 'the arch-corruptor'.[11]

However, in 1785 Horace Walpole pointed out that his father had found 'at least a great majority of every Parliament ready to take his money'. The same point was made by James Porter in 1742, 'surely if one side hath bribed, the other has done so likewise, and therefore one is as guilty of corruption as the other, as long as men are men in England, and corrupt ones too, they certainly will take money, if others will give'. That year, Sir James Lowther MP complained: 'People are so sordid and rapacious there is hardly anything but corruption from the highest to the lowest. It has been Sir Robert's masterpiece to make it . . . universal.'[12]

Walpole did not invent corruption, neither was he the originator of the system of ministerial patronage. Any such argument would insult the intelligence of predecessors, such as Harley and Sunderland, whose capacity for intrigue and for manipulating the patronage structure was substantial. Walpole was different because the longevity of his ministry, a product of political circumstances and of his more skilful and ruthless use of patronage, permitted him to be more systematic and thorough in his control of government patronage, and because this longevity and the minister's seeming invulnerability itself aroused outrage. There was a dark side to Walpole's manipulation of power. Legal and extra-legal pressures were used ruthlessly against opponents such as Opposition publishers. The Secret Office of the Post Office opened Opposition politicians' mail systematically and was not simply an anti-Jacobite precaution. These activities could only go so far, but Walpole showed no apparent reluctance to use them. Charles Erskine, a Scottish critic, wrote in 1742 that Walpole's administration should be:

offensive to every true Briton, by his endeavouring by bribery and corruption, and promises and threatenings, to tempt or awe a free people into a slavish dependence upon him, and a sacrificing their natural right and freedom, of which I had myself a pretty strong proof in the year 1734, when I got a message brought me in the name of a great man assuring me, that I should not have nor keep anything of the Government if I voted for any person in opposition to the person set up by the Court, to which my answer was, that I was till then undetermined whom I would vote for, but that the message had determined me to vote against any man whom they who sent such a message should set up for; and falling also about that time to be a Member of Assembly, I got also a message assuring me that if I did not vote for the Moderator proposed by the Court I could not have nor keep anything of the government, and as I gave the same answer to this message as I gave to the other, and acted accordingly in both cases, so the threatening which was sent me was soon fulfilled

and he was dismissed from his official position.[13]

There was widespread concern about the idea of a prime or sole minister. The Opposition Whig Samuel Sandys told the Commons in February 1741 that 'sole minister [was] a name and thing unknown to England or any free nations, but taken from a neighbouring nation', presumably France. The notion of a prime minister was attacked in Opposition publications. One stated in 1747 that: 'The King, according to the British Constitution, is the sole Prime Minister: No subject can execute that power for him without danger to our liberties.'[14] The Swedish envoy Count Sparre reported in June 1733 that though Walpole had 'great capacity and affability', he had 'not been able to escape so great a hatred; but then he has likewise much contributed to it himself by pretending contrary to the genius of this nation, to be absolute in his Ministry', which, according to Sparre, was contrary to British history and practices.[15]

However, given the absence of party discipline, the distribution of places and pensions was the only way of enabling the ministry to gain the co-operation of Parliament; it provided the link between executive and legislature. It was partly their realisation of this that led the Opposition politicians under Carteret and Pulteney, who gained office when Walpole fell, to discard the reform programme directed against places and pensions that they had advocated whilst in opposition. Walpole's methods were continued throughout the century. 'Junius', the bitter critic of the Duke of Grafton's ministry, claimed in the *Public Advertiser* of 8 July 1769 that 'in the common arts of domestic corruption, we miss no part of Sir Robert Walpole's system except his abilities'.

Walpole himself made vast gains from his years in office and he flaunted his wealth to a degree that offended many. His son Robert's marriage in 1724 was described as: 'the most splendid wedding has been in England these many years . . . it makes money circulate for Mr. Walpole has been more than ordinary generous on this occasion and bought all with ready money more like a prince than a commoner.'[16] He spent vast sums of money on building a palatial country seat at Houghton in Norfolk. No expense had been spared, noted an impressed Lord Hervey in 1727. Five years later the Duchess of Kent wrote that Walpole's green velvet bed for Houghton was 'so richly embroidered with gold as to cost some thousand pounds'. The house was filled with some of the finest paintings in Europe to form a collection that surpassed the descriptive power of one visitor in 1756. The Attorney General, Sir Dudley Ryder, finding Walpole with a new painting when he visited him in 1739, noted in his diary: 'I find pictures are a sort of mistress and his foible. He owns it himself that he cannot see a fine picture and be easy till he has it.'[17] The means by which Walpole accumulated his wealth were criticised. It was common for the Opposition to publicise the places held by his family and the Tory MP Edward Harley estimated that the annual worth of the 'places held by the Walpole family when Lord Orford asked and accepted a pension of £4000 out of the Excise' was £28,000.[18]

Walpole realised, as Henry Pelham was to do in 1746–54, that the utilisation of the patronage resources of the Crown combined with the avoidance of contentious legislation, could help to ensure ministerial stability. There was little to fear from the electorate, for even if the ministry was generally unsuccessful in the larger 'open' constituencies, the counties and the large cities, such as Bristol and London, they could rely on a large number of the 'pocket boroughs', seats that were controlled or heavily influenced by patrons. Some 'pocket boroughs', such as Amersham, Marlborough and Newton, were controlled by Tory families, while Hedon was dominated by William Pulteney, but most were at the disposal of the Whigs or heavily influenced by the government. In the 1741 general election it was to be the defection from the ministry of a number of patrons – Frederick, Prince of Wales, the Duke of Argyll, Lord Falmouth and George Dodington – that led to a result that reduced Walpole's majority to an unacceptably low level. Walpole was helped by the fact that, thanks to the Septennial Act, he only had to fight four elections as leading minister of the crown: 1722, 1727, 1734 and 1741.[19]

Walpole and the first two Georges

The principal threat to a minister came not from the electorate, but from those who might contest his control of ministerial and royal patronage: his colleagues and the king. Much about Walpole's ministerial longevity can be explained by reference to his relations with these men. Walpole was not George I's favourite minister and in 1721 Carteret kept up his spirits and sought to preserve Newcastle's support for Sunderland by informing him that 'The King is resolved that Walpole shall not govern, but it is hard to be prevented'.[20] Walpole's early ascendancy owed much to chance: the financial crisis of 1720 and the deaths of Stanhope and Sunderland in 1721 and 1722. His success in the session of 1721 in performing the difficult task of defending Whig involvement in the South Sea Company consolidated Walpole's position as the leading ministerial spokes-man in the Commons. He was to maintain this position until 1742, thanks to his refusal to follow the usual course of successful politicians, such as Harley, Bolingbroke and Stanhope, and obtain promotion to the Lords. As government manager and principal spokesman in the Commons and a skilled finance minister, Walpole was invaluable to George I, though it is unclear whether the king would have supported him against Sunderland in the rift that was prevented only by the latter's sudden death from pleurisy. In July 1723 Townshend claimed that the recent successful parliamentary session and the revival of credit had helped Walpole and himself with George. The following month Walpole congratulated himself on accurately predicting financial movements for George and on the flourishing condition of public credit, 'I think 'tis plain we shall have the whole supply of next year at 3 per cent'. In 1721 Bishop Gibson had claimed that 'as long as our great men go on to agree among themselves, all is like to go very well'. However, this was not to be.[21] Walpole had to struggle hard in 1724–5 to remove from power his opponents within the ministry, Cadogan, Carteret, Macclesfield and Roxburgh. In late 1723 Carteret had 'great hopes from Cadogan and Roxburgh's being able to form a party', but in practice the removal of Walpole's ministerial rivals did not lead to problems in Parliament.[22] With time Walpole appears to have earned the respect of George I, but he cannot be described fairly as the prime minister in George's last years: he never enjoyed sufficient influence with George, and Townshend's authority in the field of foreign policy was clearly independent of Walpole. There is, however, no truth in the reports which circulated in 1727 that George I had planned to disgrace Walpole shortly before his death.[23]

George II's accession threatened to bring about Walpole's fall. It was very rare for the leading minister of one monarch to be retained by his successor. Indeed in 1726 one Jacobite commentator claimed that the future George II would disgrace and execute Walpole and, urging that the Jacobites should therefore approach Walpole, suggested Shippen for the task.[24] On 3 June 1727, eight days before the death of George I, the London newspaper *Applebee's Original Weekly Journal* published a letter warning 'all designing statesmen, and unwary politicians' that:

> as their power only depends upon the breath of their sovereigns, an angry blast of that flings them at once from the summit of their glory, and height of their ambition; or, at most, their authority generally determines with the life of their Prince, it being very rarely found that the most expert statesman can continue a favourite to two Princes successively.

George came to the throne determined to be his own master. The Lord Chancellor, Lord King, wrote, 'The King, when he came to the throne, had formed a system both of men and things'. The replacement of Walpole by Spencer Compton, Treasurer to George as Prince of Wales, and Speaker of the Commons, appeared likely for several days after the accession. Walpole managed to survive the crisis, partly because of Compton's lack of political skills and partly because the new queen, Caroline, supported the minister, as she was to do until her death in 1737. Arthur Onslow MP noted:

> that everybody expected, that Mr. Compton the Speaker would be the Minister, and Sir Robert Walpole thought so too, for a few days . . . the new King's first inclination and resolution, which

> were certainly for Mr. Compton. . . . It went so far as to be almost
> a formal appointment, the King, for two or three days directing
> everybody to go to him upon business . . . but by the Queen's
> management, all this was soon over-ruled.

Lord King's account of Compton's failure did not mention the queen, but suggested that George was persuaded, by private experience, to continue Walpole in power, 'by his constant application to the King by himself in the mornings, when the Speaker, by reason of the sitting of the House of Commons, was absent, he so worked upon the King, that he not only established himself in favour with him, but prevented the cashiering of many others'.[25]

There were several obvious reasons why it would have been foolish to remove Walpole. The accession of a new monarch meant that Parliament had to be summoned, the Civil List settled and elections held for a new Parliament. The elections were a triumph for Walpole. After the petitions had been heard, the new House consisted of 415 ministerial supporters, 15 Opposition Whigs and 128 Tories, a government majority of 272, the largest since George I's accession. In addition, Britain's ally France pressed George II to maintain Walpole in power.[26] The Saxon envoy, Le Coq, reported that Walpole's influence with Parliament and with the great chartered companies – the Bank of England, East India Company and South Sea Company – was held to be very important for the creditworthiness and stability of the government.[27]

Despite his success, Walpole's position was weakened by the fact that George II's accession led to the entry into office of courtiers with whom the king was closely associated, such as Compton, ennobled as Earl of Wilmington, and the earls of Chesterfield and Scarborough. Further difficulty was created in 1729 when the two Secretaries of State, Townshend and the Duke of Newcastle, fell out whilst Townshend and Walpole seriously disagreed over foreign policy. These ministerial difficulties were resolved in two crises, one in 1730 which saw the resignation of Townshend and the removal from office of Carteret,[28] the other in 1733 when Chesterfield, Wilmington, Scarborough and other ministerial Whigs failed to drive Walpole from office during the Excise crisis. Instead he was able to force them into opposition, as with Chesterfield and Stair, or acquiescence, as with Wilmington and Townshend's replacement, the Earl of Harrington.

It has been suggested that the expulsion from the ministry of men of talent weakened it. This may well be true, and one can note Sarah Marlborough's barbed comment of 1740: 'Sir Robert . . . never likes any but fools, and such as have lost all credit. . . . I cannot reckon above two in the administration that have common sense.'[29] However, the expulsion also served to increase the stability of the ministry. The presence of figures such as Chesterfield, who had been willing to intrigue actively with sections of the Opposition, had been a disruptive force. The political tensions of the periods 1714–17, 1720–1 and 1742–4 when no individual minister wielded power comparable to that of Walpole in the 1730s suggest that his determination to dominate the government should not be seen as a source of ministerial instability. Walpole was probably at the peak of his power at Court and in the ministry in 1734–8. He survived the Excise crisis of 1733, the high point of the Opposition campaign against him, to win the general election of 1734. The Excise certainly handicapped ministerial candidates. 'The excise scheme is made a handle of everywhere' noted a leading newsletter, while in Kent Sir George Oxenden, one of the Lords of the Treasury, 'had a most terrible weight to struggle with, that of the Excise'. One commentator claimed that 'there has not been such a cross-grained medley of an election for the last 50 years' and that Oxenden, who was defeated, was a bad candidate, 'it should have been one not liable to the excise clamour'.[30] Walpole's majority fell from 272 to 102: 330 ministerial supporters, 83 Opposition Whigs and 145 Tories being elected. However, it was sufficient to enable him to govern easily, and the next election was not due until 1741, which gave time for place and patronage to do their work.

Despite differing with George II over British policy in the War of the Polish Succession (1733–5), Walpole retained the support, indeed the affection, of the king. The attempt to create a country party encountered increasing difficulties due to tension and differences of opinion between the Tories and the Opposition Whigs, and in 1735 Bolingbroke left the country in despair. There was little co-ordination of parliamentary tactics between the two groups. Walpole was clearly the dominant force in the ministry. The Austrian diplomat Wasner reported in 1734 that he was the minister on whom all the others depended absolutely, and two years later that he governed the country alone, the Secretaries of State simply executing his orders. In 1735 the Sardinian envoy Ossorio wrote that he was the sole source of all that was done in the kingdom.[31] The Opposition were disappointed in their hope that Walpole would fall after the death of Caroline in 1737. In 1731 Pulteney had in the Commons 'alluded to the report that Sir Robert Walpole is only supported by the Queen'. The contrast between Caroline's bright, sparkling, witty nature and George's more dour, boorish demeanour greatly influenced contemporaries and led commentators such as the courtier Lord Hervey to present George as manipulated by Caroline and Walpole. In 1720 Lady Cowper observed that the future king 'is governed by the Princess as she is by Walpole'. In November 1727 Walpole, telling Lord King 'of the great credit he had with the king', attributed it to 'the means of the Queen, who was the most able woman to govern in the world'. However, though Caroline earned a reputation as a skilful intriguer, it is possible to suggest that her influence has been exaggerated.[32] George may have been no intellectual, but he was shrewd and able to appreciate Walpole's ability. George II promised him his continued support[33] and gave it until the end of the ministry.

The limits of management: Walpole's fall

Walpole's position deteriorated markedly in 1739. The War of Jenkins' Ear was begun with Spain despite Walpole's prediction that it would lead to major difficulties.[34] Having been criticised in 1738 and early 1739 for not being willing to fight, the ministry soon found itself facing sustained criticism both within and outside Parliament, over the unsuccessful and insufficiently glorious conduct of the war. The Opposition failed in the sessions of 1739, 1740 and 1741 to bring down the ministry, attempts which culminated on 13 February 1741 in motions in both Houses for the removal of Walpole from his Majesty's councils for ever. The Tories had not been consulted and the suspicion that most of them felt of the Opposition Whigs led many of them to vote against the motion or to abstain. Pulteney blamed their action on Jacobitism[35] while claiming that some of their leaders had promised support, but it was clear to informed contemporaries that the Tories were being made use of, and were not likely to gain much from an Opposition victory.

However, Walpole was placed under increasing difficulties as a result of divisions within the government, Newcastle challenging his foreign policy and patronage decisions. In 1740 Newcastle kept Walpole in the dark about his correspondence with Harrington, who had accompanied George II to Hanover. Furthermore, the Tories and Opposition Whigs combined effectively at the end of 1741, the former acting partly in response to instructions from the Pretender, the latter encouraged by the active opposition of Frederick, Prince of Wales. In many constituencies, the Tories and the Opposition Whigs had co-operated in the 1741 elections; 286 ministerial supporters, 131 Opposition Whigs and 136 Tories were elected, Walpole's majority falling from 42 at the end of the last Parliament to 19 due to defeats in Cornwall and Scotland. Walpole made major efforts to mobilise his support in the Commons. Placemen, such as the Scottish MP Sir James Grant, received personal letters asking them to attend the first day of the session as 'it is very probable that matters of the greatest importance will come under immediate consideration'.[36]

Walpole's inability to retain his majority reflected the refusal of a few ministerial MPs to attend debates on election petitions. As in 1733 at the time of the Excise crisis, the ministry was damaged by the abstention, rather than the outright desertion of some of its supporters. Explaining bad parliamentary news, Newcastle informed his wife, 'it was occasioned by the absence of friends', a view shared by the Earl of Morton and by Lord Hartington who noted of one crucial division, 'we lost it entirely by our own people's deserting us'.[37] Possibly Walpole could have hung on. The Opposition was divided, several of its leaders seeking an accommodation with the ministry. Co-operation between Tories and Opposition Whigs could be sustained on election petitions, but it is not clear that the Tories would have maintained their support of a united Opposition for very long. They had not done so in 1718, or in February 1741 when many had refused to support the Opposition Whig motion in the Commons for Walpole's dismissal. Furthermore, the tide of European conflict turned in favour of Austria in the winter of 1741–2, a helpful development for a ministry that had been accused by the Opposition of failing to support Austria, and thus endangering the European balance of power.

However, Walpole appears to have been not entirely unwilling to resign and retire to the House of Lords, provided that the Opposition leaders would promise not to persecute him after his departure. He was old and unwell, and the strain of managing the Commons was beginning to tell, but he had not forgotten his time in the Tower 30 years before. In February 1740 Walpole told Dudley Ryder that:

> he would certainly be glad to quit, but the violent opposition made it necessary for him not to turn his back, which if he did his enemies might take advantage of it and attack him with more advantage. That he had the only confidence with the King, with whom he often talked freely. That the King often showed him letters and complaints which he had received privately against him ... the King always then flew into passions against Sir Robert's enemies ... he said that he would now quit if he could put the administration of affairs into any other hand that was fit.[38]

Once the parliamentary majority of a ministry began to fall and rumours circulated of government changes, it proved very difficult to retain the loyalty of MPs keen to make bargains with those they believed were about to take power. This was a major problem for the ministry in 1733 and again in the winter of 1741–2. In February 1735, when the ministerial majority fell to 53 in a division over increasing the size of the army, Lord Perceval, by then Earl of Egmont, had noted in his diary, 'I hear the Court is not pleased at seeing so small a majority, and on this occasion Mons. Chavigny, the French Ambassador, told my son what the late Lord Sunderland once told him, namely, that whenever an English Minister had but 60 majority in the House of Commons he was undone.' Various statements were attributed to Walpole. In 1769 one newspaper claimed: 'Sir Robert Walpole used to say, that whenever the Opposition came so near as within forty, he should look on his power as lost'. The following year it was stated that Walpole had been in the habit of saying that if his majority fell below 100 he would be very concerned, but that if it fell to 50 or lower it would be time to resign.[39]

After the 1741 general election, Walpole enjoyed no such margins. In divisions on the Bossiney election petition on 9 and 11 December 1741 his majorities were only 6 and 7. Walpole was defeated on the Westminster and Denbighshire election petitions and then on 16 December on the chairmanship of the Commons' elections committee, which 'dispirited the friends of that gentleman to a great degree'.[40]

In a political world without reliable sources of information, it was essential to create the impression of being successful. Walpole was no longer able to do so by the beginning of 1742. He needed a brilliant coup, such as the reconciliation with the Prince of Wales which he sought, in order to prevent a leakage of support and remain in power. The prince refused to come to terms until his father dismissed Walpole. The prince's attitude encouraged politicians such as Dorset and Wilmington to believe that Walpole would fall and that it would be better to bargain with the leaders of the Opposition than with the minister, especially when the king was nearly 60. Egmont noted that the attempted reconciliation: 'has effectually undone [Walpole], it having fixed such members among the anti-courtiers who were wavering in their conduct, upon suspicion that the Prince might be prevailed on to reconcile himself to his Majesty, whereby his servants by going over to the Court would cast the majority of the House of Commons on the Court side, whereas this full declaration of his Royal Highness against Sir Robert, assures them he will not give them up.'[41] On 21 January 1742 Pulteney's motion for a secret committee to inquire into Walpole's administration was defeated in the Commons by three votes only. A week later Walpole lost the Chippenham election petition by one vote. The government clearly had to be reconstituted for control of Parliament to be regained and that obviously involved the resignation of Walpole.[42] Writing on 4 February 1742, George Dodington, one of Walpole's Whig opponents, saw Providence at work in his fall:

> Our labourious attendance in Parliament . . . I never saw such an attendance either in length, continuance, numbers and spirit on our side. The Union of Parties has been more than the work of Man, such steadiness, mutual affection, and cordiality must have been the Stand of Providence. Those that were called Tories, (for I thank God, we are losing all party Distinctions) have behaved in a manner so noble, so just that it must do them everlasting honour. Their country owes its safety (if it is to be saved) to their behaviour, and I doubt not but they will meet with the honour they deserve. We have overturned our adversary, he is out of all employment, and Earl of Orford, but I think not out of danger.[43]

After the fall

Resigning in February 1742, Walpole survived the attempts of a secret committee of Parliament set up to investigate him and discredit his ministry, though he took the matter so seriously that he had many of his papers burnt, thus creating a great obstacle to understanding how he worked. Sarah Marlborough was not alone in arguing that Walpole should receive a severe punishment, 'because I really think the Constitution cannot be recovered without some example being made'.[44] Officials such as Nicholas Paxton, the Solicitor to the Treasury, and John Scrope, the Secretary to the Treasury, refused to testify against Walpole. The Opposition passed a bill through the Commons to indemnify those who would testify only to see the Court majority in the Lords reject it. A leading Opposition newspaper, the *London Evening Post*, in its issue of 10 July 1742 juxtaposed the collapse of the inquiry into Walpole with an item on the death sentence for some petty thieves, adding the comment 'such is the difference of stealing a shilling or £20,000'. In January 1744 the Earl of Westmorland complained in the Lords that

Walpole had been allowed to retire from posts he had wickedly and unskilfully discharged with all the rewards of wisdom and integrity.[45] The Opposition alliance disintegrated speedily, with Carteret and Pulteney taking office in a ministry that included most of the Old Corps Whigs, the former supporters of the Walpole ministry. The Tories and certain of the Opposition Whigs complained bitterly of their abandonment by their former allies, who also neglected most of their programme for legislation against corruption. The Tory MP Edward Harley noted when the Place Bill was rejected in the Lords in April 1742, 'Lord Carteret voted against the Bill though he had always spoke for it when he was out of place'. Later that month, Harley wrote: 'Mr. Pulteney presented a bill to exclude certain officers from being members of the House of Commons. A sham bill of no use.'[46] A Tory attempt to secure the repeal of the Septennial Act was defeated in the Commons. Thomas Hay wrote from Edinburgh to the Marquis of Tweeddale, an ally of Carteret's who had been made Secretary of State for Scotland:

> in general the use that is made of such incidents here is to represent the present ministry as differing only in name from the former but really the same and pursuing the same measures in every respect and what affords a great handle for such suggestions is the keeping in place or taking the assistance of those formerly employed or in the Earl of Orford's interest though it is visible the rash and ill advised measures of some of the old opposition party who yet stand out made what has been done absolutely necessary.[47]

General disenchantment with the ratting of the Patriots, as the Opposition Whigs called themselves, led to a revival of Walpole's popularity. The possibility of his return was mentioned by several commentators. In December 1742 the London banker, Sir Matthew Decker, noted that it was generally thought that: 'my Lord Orford gets ground daily. I had last Sunday a visit of a Tory Member who was so dissatisfied with the new folks, that he protested, he was sorry he had ever given a vote against him, and went further by saying that if an address was proposed in the House, to the King, for reestablishing the said Lord he would give his vote for it, and he was sure many of his stamp would do the same, and if this should happen I shall be one of the number that shall not be surprised at it, as I am at nothing that happens in this country.' Walpole's son Horace reflected in 1745 when his father died, 'he had lived . . . to see . . . his enemies brought to infamy for their ignorance or villainy, and the world allowing him to be the only man in England fit to be what he had been'. Horace added in 1748: 'what ample revenge every year gives my father against his Patriot enemies! Had he never deserved well himself, posterity must still have the greatest opinion of him, when they see on what rascal foundations were built all the pretences to virtue, which was set up in opposition to him.'[48]

After his fall, Walpole was believed to retain considerable influence with George II, a position similar to that which Lord Bute was believed to hold with George III after his resignation in 1763. It was always simpler to castigate royal views by blaming them on a supposedly evil adviser. In the case of Walpole it was true that he exercised considerable influence on George from his retirement until his death on 18 March 1745. George sought and valued his advice, and Walpole played a major role in ensuring that in the ministerial rivalry of the period his former protégé Henry Pelham triumphed over his former rivals, Pulteney and Carteret. The Earl of Wilmington (formerly Spencer Compton) had succeeded Walpole at the Treasury. When he died in July 1743 Pelham beat Pulteney, now Earl of Bath, for the post. The absence in 1742–4 of a minister wielding power comparable to that of Walpole helped to exacerbate tension. In September 1743 Newcastle stated that he, Pelham and Hardwicke wished:

> to act with Lord Carteret, with confidence and friendship, provided he really acts in the same manner towards us; but it must be upon the foot of equality and not superiority, of mutual confidence and communication, in all things, as well foreign, as domestic. This is the only way for the King's business to be carried on with ease and success to ourselves and the public. A contrary behaviour must create coolness and diffidence amongst us, tend to division, and the forming separate parties, the consequence of which, must

prove the ruin of the one or the other, and be the destruction of the King's affairs.[49]

Given this attitude it was not surprising that Walpole told Dudley Ryder that 'the Pelhams and Chancellor treat the King in an imprudent manner, not submissive enough, though the King piques himself on not having anybody to dictate to him'.[50] Walpole was very opposed to the new idea of a broadly based ministry that would include Tories. On 2 February 1742, two days after he had decided to retire, Walpole wrote to the Duke of Devonshire: 'I am of opinion that the Whig party must be kept together, which may be done with this parliament, if a Whig administration be formed.'[51] Pelham continued Walpole's policy, rejecting in the autumn of 1743 Chesterfield's pressure for a mixed ministry: 'he will not take in the few Torys proposed, upon the Coalition, but only upon a personal foot, and that even he would rather have them without their followers, than with, for fear of offending the old Whig corps.'[52] Walpole gave Pelham advice on parliamentary management and on patronage, stressing the importance of the Treasury. In 1744 he played a major role in rallying the Whigs in support of the payment of subsidies for the Hanoverian forces, an object dear to George II's heart although politically contentious. Philip Yorke MP noted, 'Lord Orford certainly took great pains to bring all his friends into the measure', while the Tory MP Edward Harley claimed that: 'the question for the Hanover troops was carried in both Houses by the influence and management of Sir Robert Walpole now Earl of Orford.'[53] For the first time since becoming a peer Walpole spoke in Parliament on this subject on 24 February 1744. He revealed over the issue his continuing belief that stability depended on a strong Whig party acting in Parliament in support of the Protestant succession.

Pelham's policies during his ministry, which lasted, with a brief interruption in 1746, until his death in 1754, represented a continuation of those of Walpole: fiscal restraint, pacific foreign policy, unenterprising legislation, not disturbing the status quo in the Church, a Whig monopoly of power. Helped by a peaceful international situation and by the longevity of George II, Pelham was able to enjoy substantial parliamentary majorities and govern successfully.[54] Walpole's policies neither fell nor failed with the man.

Patronage

Patronage was ubiquitous in eighteenth-century Britain. Patronage networks were a social feature of the age, often controlled by private citizens for socio-economic as well as for political purposes, and not merely the aberrant creation of Crown and ministers. Apart from the clientage systems of landed magnates and borough-mongers, patronage relationships of one kind or another were also involved in the gentry's control of parochial appointments in the Church; their bestowing land tenures based on favourable leases, or with the contingent suspension of onerous terms; the commercial relationships between wealthier members of the community and the merchants and artisans whose products and services they consumed; the distribution of commissions and contracts to architects, builders and civil engineers by city corporations as well as by aristocratic patrons; the control exercised by bishops, deans and chapters over both property and benefices; and even the appointment of parish pump officials (constables, church wardens, overseers of the poor) by the influence of social superiors.

The key to Walpole's ministerial longevity was not simply his policies. Much was due to his skills in parliamentary management and his control of government patronage. As the Duke of Portland observed in 1725, 'he never does anything for nothing'.[55] A French memorandum of 1736 claimed that whilst Walpole had control over patronage he would enjoy a secure parliamentary majority, and that whilst he had a majority he would retain his control over patronage. According to the memorandum this circle would be very difficult for the Opposition to break, particularly if peace were maintained, a timely reminder of the need to relate patronage and policy. Newcastle wrote of the newly-elected Parliament in 1734, 'it will require great care, attention, and management to set out right, and keep people in good humour'.[56] Confronted by a veritable onslaught of demands for the benefits of patronage – places (offices) and pensions (cash payments) – Walpole was very astute at managing the patronage resources at his disposal.

As head of the Treasury he was at the centre of the network of government patronage, although there were spheres, particularly the army, Church and Scotland, where his influence was limited, due to the role of other patrons, the king, Gibson and the Earl of Ilay respectively. That did not mean that Walpole was without influence in these fields. His account of a discussion with Gibson about filling vacant bishoprics in 1723 was very detailed and senior clerics clearly thought it worth their while to seek his support: 'The Bishop of Hereford has wrote to me most strongly to go to Ely.' Patronage occupied much of Walpole's time. Most of his meetings with the king concerned patronage and a large portion of his surviving correspondence was devoted to the same issue.[57] The wide-ranging nature of Walpole's influence, the role of aristocratic support and the complicated permutations that patronage decisions gave rise to are illustrated by a letter of 1726 from Richard Arundell to his friend the 3rd Earl of Burlington, on whose interest he sat, without a contest, as MP for Knaresborough from 1720 with his death in 1758. In 1726 the post of Surveyor General of Works became vacant: 'upon which Sir Robert Walpole recommended me to the King, who has consented to give me [the] Employment. Great endeavours have been used to make Kent Comptroller, tho' to no effect, and he (Sir Robert) told me yesterday that he was obliged to make Ripley Comptroller to obviate the Duke of Devonshire's recommendation, and remove Howard from the Board, who is to have Dartiquenave's place, and Dartiquenave the Gardens and that he had spoke to the King to put Kent into Ripley's employment which was agreed to.' William Kent, a protégé of Burlington's, had carried out decorative work at Kensington Palace for George I before beginning work at Houghton for Walpole.[58]

Walpole also featured most regularly in the correspondence of others by virtue of his role in patronage. In 1737 the prominent Cumbrian Whig, Viscount Lonsdale, wrote to Sir George Fleming, the Bishop of Carlisle, to assure him that he was happy to see the latter's nephew obtain a vacant post in the Customs at Whitehaven. However, he added:

> But for my own part I can't contribute at all towards it, for as I have no reason to think that any of these employments would be given upon my request, t'would be very unfitting for me to ask for them. Might I take the liberty of advising your Lordship you should write directly to Sir Robert Walpole, for 'tis he alone that disposes of all these places, and expects application for them to be made to himself.

Walpole had constantly to disappoint with care, being mindful of the political implications of his actions. In June 1731, John Drummond and Robert Douglas, both MPs, pressed Walpole to obtain a commission in the army for the latter. Walpole assured Douglas: 'that he should be provided for in course, and that it should be done with all the dispatch that could be, but that he behoved to have patience till his turn came which he hoped would be soon.' The impatient Douglas waited again in September on Walpole: 'who has given him fresh assurances of being provided for, the young Gentleman looked a little surly. Sir Robert told him that young men always walked faster than old men.' Douglas was in fact promoted to captain the following year. This promotion, however, bound him to Walpole, for in 1735 the latter was able to threaten him with its loss when he was dissatisfied with the captain's vote in the Commons.

Whether he convinced suppliants or not, they generally had to accept what he told them. Charles Cathcart reported of a meeting with Walpole in 1716: 'I pressed him hard for the £500 to my sister in law, he made a merit of his having agreed to the £200, when as he said the King had rejected the thing entirely. I do not believe one word of this, but it was by no means proper to let him into that secret.' A suppliant observing the pressure Walpole was under reflected in 1738, 'you are not much to be envied'.[59] Five years later Sir William Yonge MP, one of Walpole's principal spokesmen in the Commons and an office-holder who survived his patron's fall, provided evidence of the pressure for patronage. As Secretary at War, a post he held from 1735 under 1746, he wrote to Carteret:

Though I have always had an inclination to favour the Colonels with regard to their recommendations of ensigns and second lieutenants, yet I beg leave to observe on this occasion that the great number of vacancies have occasioned strong solicitations from noblemen and gentlemen of weight and interest in their several counties, and by the long time they have been indisposed of, they are become very importunate and uneasy. I should therefore hope His Majesty would at this time have a more particular regard to recommendations of this nature ... among these John Fletcher recommended by Sir James Lowther I must name particularly.[60]

Such comments reveal the importance of regarding patronage as an integral part of the social system rather than as simply a political mechanism. They therefore suggest that Opposition complaints of political manipulation require a measure of qualification in terms of prevailing social norms and pressures. However, there is little doubt of the outrage that lay behind many of these complaints. One of the leading Opposition London newspapers complained that the Walpole and Carteret ministries had had no 'regard for personal merit, or experience in military offices' and had made 'a pecuniary interest the only step by which the bravest, the oldest, and the ablest of our soldiers and seamen could rise to the common justice which was due to their rank and services'.[61] Such a policy could be blamed for defeats in the War of the Austrian Succession.

Many self-styled independent politicians were in fact linked to Walpole's patronage network, often seeking favours for relatives, friends, constituents and protégés. Sir James Lowther could not have maintained his electoral interest in Cumbria without help from the ministry. John Lord Perceval also prided himself on his independence. However, he relied on Walpole's help to maintain his political interest in Harwich, for which he was an MP.

Walpole and Parliament

In 1739 Walpole told the Commons: 'I have lived long enough

in the world to know, that the safety of a minister lies in his having the approbation of this House. Former ministers neglected this, and therefore they fell! I have always made it my first study to obtain it, and therefore I hope to stand.'[62] The minister devoted a lot of time to Parliament, both as a speaker and as the prime lobbyist for the ministerial cause. Sir William Gordon MP described in 1715 how Walpole, 'with a strength of reasoning and power of eloquence peculiar to himself, opened up a charge of high treason against the Lord Bolingbroke', one of the Tory leaders. Five years later Thomas Brodrick, an independent Whig MP, referred to Walpole as speaking 'with the utmost skill' and again 'with the greatest skill imaginable'. In 1722 he was described as speaking with 'extraordinary strength and weight'.[63] Chesterfield described him as: 'the best Parliament man, and the ablest manager of Parliament, that I believe ever lived. An artful rather than an eloquent speaker, he saw as if by intuition, the disposition of the House and pressed or receded accordingly.'[64] Philip Yorke, later 2nd Earl of Hardwicke, wrote of Walpole that he was 'the best House of Commons man we ever had'.[65] George II and Queen Caroline regarded him as: 'by so great a superiority the most able man in the Kingdom, that he understood the revenue, and knew how to manage that formidable and refractory body, the House of Commons, so much better than any other man, that it was impossible for the business of the crown to be well done without him.'[66] He was a good speaker, impressive on most topics and outstanding on fiscal matters. In the 1737 debate over the rate of interest to be paid on the National Debt, Walpole spoke an hour and three-quarters at one time, and 'it was allowed that there was never a finer speech made, and that he had even outshined himself it was so glorious a performance'.[67] As a lobbyist he combined his control over most ministerial patronage and his engaging affable personality, with an appreciation of what Parliament might be willing to grant. Meetings of his supporters at the Cockpit were used by Walpole to maintain unity. Mrs Caesar noted, 'no man ever had his followers at more command than has Sir Robert'.[68] A pamphlet of 1744 stated that: 'though the power of the late minister had a very broad and deep foundation, he knew his influence on the House of Commons was the cement which held all together.'[69] There were those whose support the ministry was certain of, the 'Dead Men for a Ministry', those allegedly 'ready to vote that black is white',[70] but they were not sufficient to ensure a majority. In 1739 Frederick William I of Prussia instructed his envoy in London to approach Walpole over a commercial matter, as the latter's credit was so great in the Commons that he alone was capable of determining the fate of the affair.[71]

Walpole himself was more modest about his strength. In a ministerial meeting in 1738 to discuss Spanish depredations – the Spanish attacks on British commerce in the West Indies that helped to cause the Anglo-Spanish war of 1739–48 – 'Sir Robert said it was necessary not to attempt to extenuate or alleviate the depredations; the temper of the House would not bear it.'[72] He was careful to press supporters to attend the House.[73] Walpole's lobbying was not restricted to the Commons. He was also very active in persuading particular peers to support government policy, arranging, for example, payments to Earl Coningsby in 1723 when he switched from Opposition to government. It was to Walpole that Townshend turned that year to probe the 'inclinations' of the new Earl of Bradford.[74] If it was considered inexpedient to block Opposition legislation in the Commons it could be defeated in the Lords. When a bill against bribery was considered in 1726, one MP noted, 'Sir Robert Walpole gave us to understand that nothing would come of it, intimating the little likelihood of its going through the Lords'.[75] Peers did not have to consider their constituents and the smaller House of Lords was a less volatile body than the Commons. On the other hand, Walpole had a much tougher time with the House of Lords in the 1730s, than the other two ministers of comparable ascendancy that century, Lord North and the Younger Pitt. There were closer divisions and a much narrower gap between government and Opposition proxies in the 1730s than in the 1770s or 1783–1801. Thanks to his activities Walpole was well aware of the likely response of Parliament to particular proposals, and this, as much as his manipulation of patronage, explains his success in retaining control of the legislature. This success helped to make Britain a functioning parliamentary monarchy, one in which Parliament and the Crown operated in harmony. This was a considerable achievement, and helped to ensure that Britain with its high levels, by contemporary standards, of personal and religious freedom, was praised by many continental intellectuals. To writers such as Montesquieu the British constitution was worthy of praise and deserving of imitation in some respects.

Not all foreign commentators were equally enthusiastic, some being influenced by Bolingbroke's portrayal of the Walpolean system as corrupt and unpopular.[76] Scepticism was expressed from a different perspective by British officials and ministerial writers who felt that excessive freedom for criticising and opposing the government existed. One official, George Tilson, complained in 1722 that the election for the parliamentary seat of Westminster revealed: 'a good deal of what is called English Liberty that is licentiousness. The same spirit of the elections often gets into the House among the elected. Only 500 are not so unruly quite as 5000.' Philip Yorke, the eldest son of Lord Chancellor Hardwicke, who before he was 21 had received the lucrative life sinecure of the Tellership of the Exchequer and was returned by his father as MP for Reigate, wrote in 1742 of: 'the natural fickleness of our dispositions, our readiness to find fault if everything does not succeed at the very juncture we wish it should, and the effects of a constant opposition which our annual sessions will always contribute to keep up.'[77]

Ministerial newspapers and pamphleteers argued that their Opposition counterparts were seditious in both intent and effect. They were accused of spreading lies about government policy, and of encouraging faction, an imprecise term by which opposition could be castigated and which revealed the fundamental ambivalence deeply engrained in contemporary thought about the notion of loyal opposition. The ministerial press based its constitutional arguments on the sovereignty of Parliament, denying that extra-parliamentary views should be heeded if rejected by Parliament, and claiming that most of them were manipulated and/or self-interested. The popular appeal of the Opposition was not usually denied, but their supporters were commonly presented as a fickle and foolish 'mob',[78] a group that was differentiated from the 'people'. Ministerial papers stressed the self-interest of Opposition writers, the declamatory manner and appeal to the emotions of their writing, their creation of domestic division[79] and the impossibility of ministerial perfection.[80]

An effective parliamentary monarchy, with parliamentary control over the finances of the State, had been the aim of many of the critics of the Stuarts in the seventeenth century. The Revolution Settlement of 1688–9 had created the constitutional basis for such a monarchy, but the instability of the ministries of the period 1689–1721 suggests that the political environment within which such a monarchy could be effective had not been created. Two major wars had been financed successfully, albeit with considerable difficulty,[81] in contrast to the debacle of the last Stuart war, the Third Anglo-Dutch war of 1672–4, but policy formulation and execution had been handicapped and the confidence of allies sapped by the frequent changes in government. At one level these changes were an indication of stability: power remained the monopoly of the highest social groups, and despite Tory claims to the contrary, the Whigs were a party primarily of great landowners, not of bankers and Dissenters. At another level the political instability of 1689–1721 revealed the grave limitations of the Revolution Settlement. A parliamentary monarchy could not simply be legislated into existence. It required the development of conventions and patterns of political behaviour that would permit a constructive resolution of contrary opinions within a system where there was no single source of dominant power. The slow development of these patterns was particularly serious given the fact that Britain was at war for much of the period (1689–97, 1702–13, 1718–20) and that Jacobitism was a significant force.

3

THE CROWN AND THE POLITICAL NATION

Walpole and the Crown

The Walpole ministry was of great importance in the development of an effective constitutional monarchy. Irresponsible opposition, such as that which Walpole himself had conducted in 1717–20 and which his propaganda subsequently distorted, persisted. Opposition leaders, such as Pulteney, Wyndham and Bolingbroke, intrigued with envoys of powers hostile to Britain, in order to harm the ministry. A sizeable portion of the Tory party continued to consider Jacobitism as an option and some conspired actively for that cause. Walpole managed, however, to convince the Crown that a parliamentary monarchy could help it to achieve most of its aims, and the nation that it could provide stability, continuity, peace and lower taxes.

The education of the monarchs was of particular importance. William III and George I had created considerable difficulties by their determination to use British resources to further their own extra-British foreign policy goals, and to favour those ministers such as Stanhope and Sunderland, who would support them in this aim. Walpole's ministry saw a tempering of this habit. George I and George II were able to influence policy in favour of Hanover, but not to direct it.[1] Ministers whom the Crown favoured, largely for their views on foreign policy, were removed, against the wishes of the king, because they did not enjoy the support of Walpole, and because their policies were not likely to gain parliamentary approval. Whereas Stanhope and Sunderland had not fallen in 1717, Carteret was demoted in 1724 and Townshend resigned six years later. The very fact that two Secretaries of State, the ministers concerned with foreign policy, should depart in accordance with the wishes of the First Lord of the Treasury indicated the willingness of the Crown to accept the implications of parliamentary monarchy, although in each case Walpole only obtained his goal with considerable difficulty. For similar reasons George I maintained Walpole in power in 1727 and did not appoint his 'favourite', Spencer Compton, in his place. To have made this change would have been to follow usual practice, particularly on the Continent, but George accepted that Walpole's command of a parliamentary majority made him indispensable to the Crown. Had Compton been given control of ministerial patronage he could have sought to maintain the harmony between Crown and Parliament that had been so evident in recent sessions. However, despite his considerable parliamentary experience (as Speaker of the Commons since 1715), this might have been very difficult had Walpole gone into Opposition. Much would have depended on the policies that George II and Compton might have adopted, of which there is no indication. Walpole's move into Opposition in 1717 had been so dangerous because George I, Stanhope and Sunderland supported contentious constitutional, ecclesiastical and foreign policies. Even then, determined royal support of Stanhope and Sunderland, ministerial skill in gaining Opposition leaders such as Argyll, and a ministerial willingness to abandon contentious legislation, prevented Walpole from overthrowing the ministry in 1717–20. It is possible that the age of Walpole could have been truncated in 1727 had George II supported Compton. However, the political crisis that might have developed might also have put paid to any notion of an age of parliamentary stability.

George II was a firm believer in defending his personal position and in the 1740s he showed himself capable both of supporting a minister who did not possess a secure parliamentary position (Carteret) and of seeking to follow a personal, secret foreign policy, a British version of the French *secret du roi*.[2] This was to cause considerable instability, both within the ministry, where the Pelhams and the retired Walpole resisted Carteret, and within the political nation, where the Hanoverian issue was pushed to the fore as it had not been in the 1720s and 1730s. The latter was particularly dangerous as war brought French support for Jacobitism. Care was necessary in the handling of George II as Richard Grenville MP noted after his patron Viscount Cobham accepted military office in the summer of 1742. Grenville wrote to his naval brother Thomas:

> Lord Cobham bid me tell Mr. Haddock that if either of his sons were for the army, everything in his power should be done, and swore by God he'd jump over the moon if possible to serve him. However things must subside before the new servants can have any great weight, none of us should like to have coachmen, stewards, chamberlains, cooks etc. enter our house by force, and turn out those old ones we have long had confidence in. They must at least convince us that they have put our estates, kitchens, stables etc. into better order than the old ones kept them, before we should appoint every postilion, scullion etc. by their direction.[3]

Walpole's success during the 1720s and 1730s owed much to his ability to persuade George I and George II to accept the consequences of parliamentary monarchy. This achievement has appeared more impressive of late as recent scholarship has stressed the continued vitality, influence and power of the eighteenth-century British monarchs, and their ability to achieve many of their aims despite significant domestic opposition.[4] There was also considerable respect for the royal position although this respect did not prevent opposition. In August 1717 General Thomas Erle, long-standing MP for Wareham, explained his views to James Craggs:

> The King is certainly master of choosing who he thinks fit to employ. Those who would force others upon him, would think it hard usage to be treated so themselves in their particular concerns. I am under no apprehension but that both him and the public will be well served by those who are now in the administration. No one doubts their capacity. But there are so many who will be judges of their own, that the contention here, who shall have the power and the profit, will never be at an end. It is always happy

for England when the people are possessed, that the King governs them himself. They have always had, and always will have submission for the Crown which they never will have for one another, whilst we are divided into parties as we are. No honest man will come into measures to compel the King to employ any one, let his capacity be what it will, nor to distress those employed, out of peevishness to the person. But if the Public is apparently in danger by evil counsell the cry will then be general; and there are many instances how fatal it has been to our Kings when they have been tenacious of a favourite, who has justly incurred the odium of his subjects. God be thanked that cannot be the case now. We are governed by a wise and experienced Prince who knows how to choose and when to dismiss, according as he is served.[5]

However, Erle's support for Walpole, then in Opposition, led to his being forced to resign all his posts in March 1718.

As the role of the monarch, and therefore of the Court, in eighteenth-century politics has been re-evaluated, this has led to the need for a more sophisticated appreciation of the nature and workings of the political system. The avoidance of a clash between Crown and ministry during the Walpole period cannot simply be explained by reference to Walpole's success in meeting the Crown's financial needs through obtaining parliamentary support for a generous Civil List, the annual grant paid to the Crown by Parliament, though this was of great importance for the avaricious George II. In 1727 the king was guaranteed an annual sum of £800,000, an unprecedentedly large sum for the start of a reign.

The Crown was constrained in its freedom of political manoeuvre by the consequences of the party conflict. This made it very difficult for William III and Anne to create mixed ministries of Whigs and Tories, for the growth of party loyalty led party leaders to resign from or refuse to accept office because the monarch employed men of another party. This has led Roberts to argue recently that 'in later Stuart England the power of party overwhelmed the power of patronage'.[6] This argument is of considerable importance for the early Hanoverian period. Though Colley has claimed that the Tories were keen to serve the Crown and that George I and George II were willing to turn to the Tories, there is little evidence after 1715 for the second contention and the first probably underrates the role of Jacobite sympathies. Both kings detested the Tories as the party whose ministry had negotiated the Peace of Utrecht in 1713, ending the War of the Spanish Succession and abandoning Britain's allies, including Hanover. The Utrecht issue was used by the Whigs to great effect throughout the period 1713–40 to discredit the Tories. George I and George II suspected, and were urged to do so by the Whigs, that the Tories were inclined to support Jacobitism. The monarchs were opposed to the 'little Englander' stance of the Tories: their opposition to continental commitments, an isolationism that threatened Hanover, and their hostility to continental Protestantism. In these areas Tory prejudices and ideology, as well as Tory policies, conflicted with royal interests.

Given this situation it is not surprising that George I and George II had little time for the Tories. In 1714 the French envoy reported that George II, then Prince of Wales, would 'not suffer the sight of any Tories, regarding them all as Jacobites'. In July 1721 Newcastle wrote that:

> the report of the Tories coming in, having reached the King's ears, he has been so good as to declare to me and many other of his servants the concern he has at the report, and has assured us that he neither has or ever had any such thoughts, and is determined to stand by the Whigs, and not take in any one single Tory. He is very sensible the Whig Party is the only security he has to depend on, in which he is most certainly right, for it is impossible for his Government ever to be supported by any other Party. . . . Could I imagine there was any design to introduce the Tories I should be as much alarmed as anybody for I shall always think it destructive to the King and the Government'.[7]

At times of political tension, as in 1717 and the mid 1740s, when the monarchs risked the defeat of their favoured ministers, Stanhope and Carteret, they were prepared to threaten that they would turn to the Tories for support, but there was little substance to these threats. For practical purposes George I and George II were party monarchs, whose wish to have Whig ministries represented a constraint on their political freedom of manoeuvre. However, it did not oblige them to have a particular set of Whig ministers. The divisions within the Whig party, accentuated from 1714 onwards by political success and the consequent struggle for office and dominance, gave the monarch considerable freedom in his choice of ministers. There were essentially two types of Whig internal dispute. Disputes within the ministry were very significant, and usually involved disagreements over both policy and patronage. The conflict between Walpole and the former Sunderland group, led by Carteret and Cadogan, in 1722–4 related to disagreements over foreign policy as much as to a struggle for pre-eminence. They were inextricably intertwined as both involved an attempt to win royal support.

The second type of dispute was usually a consequence of the first. It was a formal parliamentary opposition by Whigs to the Whig ministry, such as that mounted by Walpole in 1717–20 and by Pulteney in 1726–42. These oppositions often looked to the Tories for parliamentary support, but they differed fundamentally from Tory opposition, both in that there was a good chance that the opponents would be taken back into office, and that they were linked often to ministerial factions. The great failure of the Pulteney opposition to Walpole was not the inability to defeat him in Parliament, but the failure to unite with those ministers who were opposed to Walpole. In 1730 Walpole would have been in particular difficulty had Carteret, Townshend and Wilmington supported Pulteney. Their failure to do so allowed Walpole to tackle the parliamentary and ministerial crises of 1730 separately.

In 1733 the situation was more serious as Bolton, Chesterfield, Cobham and Stair, riding a wave of popular opposition, proved willing to co-operate with the Whig Opposition in pressing for the removal of Walpole. This led in that session to the ministry facing a serious crisis in the Lords. Of the seventy-five peers who voted for the Court on 24 May 1733, Walpole's first defeat in the Lords as chief minister, only ten were without office or place. He was saved by George II's determination to support him, which helped to divide the Court opposition to Walpole, for Harrington, Scarborough and Wilmington were unwilling to push their opposition in the face of royal disapproval. In August 1733 John Drummond MP wrote of 'the destruction of Sir Robert, which is not like to happen, for I never saw him easier at Court'.[8]

Thus, despite being restricted to Whig ministries, George I and George II possessed considerable freedom as a result of Whig disputes. The Crown was the arbiter of these disputes and the court the principal sphere in which they were conducted. The ministers needed royal support, and as a result, the Crown was able to obtain considerable benefits: an enhanced Civil List, a larger army than would probably have otherwise existed, and support for Hanoverian interests, such as the subsidy treaty with Hessen-Kassel, by which Hessian troops destined for the defence of Hanover were paid by Britain and not by Hanover.[9] Furthermore, the monarchs did not always heed ministerial wishes concerning patronage. In one such matter in 1738 the Earl of Malton was informed that although Walpole had pressed George II, 'he had the misfortune and concern to find that he could not prevail'.[10]

Given this situation there was potential for a serious conflict between Crown and ministry. Neither possessed sufficient strength to dominate the other and the constitutional guidelines that sought to define their relationship, such as the Act of Settlement of 1701, were vague, providing scant guidance for most political eventualities, and dependent upon mutual good-will. There was as yet no received understanding of such central issues as the collective responsibility of the Cabinet, the particular responsibility of the departmental head, the special role of the first minister and the notion that the king should choose his ministers from those who had the confidence of Parliament.[11] Crown–ministry relations were a significant source of political instability, in ministerial and parliamentary terms, in 1716–20 and 1743–6.[12] Walpole's success in avoiding this situation was a testimony to his political skills, his attention to Court intrigue, his personal good relations with George II, and to the political responsibility of George I and George II. Hatton's biography of the former has taught us to be aware of George I's political skills and sense of responsibility, but there has been scant appreciation of George II. Too often assessments of this monarch, particularly for the Walpole period, are based on the hostile views of Lord Hervey, a courtier who disliked the king personally and wrote of him as if he were a boorish fool.[13] Recent work would suggest that this was not the case and that George, if no intellectual, was nevertheless a monarch of considerable shrewdness and political skill.[14] An incompetent and unyielding monarch might well have led to the end of Hanoverian rule in Britain.

The role of the Crown in politics and in patronage ensured that Walpole's position as leading minister was not identical with what was subsequently to become understood as the position of Prime Minister. Walpole was not supported by collective ministerial responsibility or party discipline. Ministers often saw the king individually, and, if they followed royal orders, could hope for the monarch's support against the criticism of their colleagues. The ministry and the Court usually contained members who were opposed to the leading minister and whom it was impossible for him to discipline, such as the Wilmington–Dorset–Dodington group. Given this situation and the large areas of patronage over which he had little control, it might appear surprising that Walpole's position was seen by contemporaries as a new development or that he has been regarded subsequently as the first Prime Minister. This partly reflects the vitality of opposition propaganda. Walpole paid dearly for the fact that his cultural appreciation and patronage were directed towards paintings rather than literature. The disgruntled literary talent that wrote for the Opposition presented his ministry as an aberration, a unique concentration of power reflecting evil intentions and corrupt practices. In fact Walpole's power was not unique. There had been other great ministers before him who had combined great influence at Court, control over royal patronage and responsibility for parliamentary management. The term Prime Minister, and others of a comparable nature, were applied to two of Anne's leading ministers: Lord Godolphin and Robert Harley, Earl of Oxford.[15] Walpole's position seemed novel largely because his longevity, his ability to survive the accession of a new monarch, and the degree of his influence in Court and Parliament and over patronage were outside the experience of all living commentators, and because so much attention was devoted to it.

The claims that Walpole's position represented a new departure ignored the absence of any institutional change affecting his position as minister. Early eighteenth-century Britain was not an age of administrative revolution. Such innovation as took place was largely in fiscal matters and in the government of Scotland after the Union of 1707, and not in the reorganisation of ministerial responsibilities. Just as there was no simplification of the system by which two Secretaries of State shared responsibility for foreign policy and for law and order until 1782,[16] so there was no clarification of the role, powers and responsibilities of the leading minister. This was not surprising, given the widespread hostility to the idea of such a position, but it left unclear such matters as whether the leading minister was supposed to sit in the Commons or the Lords, be a Secretary of State or the First Lord of the Treasury. There were benefits from such a flexible, inchoate system, but the absence of definition also served to increase greatly the scope for ministerial strife, and this was to be particularly serious after the fall of Walpole. It would, therefore, be mistaken to suggest that Walpole created the office of Prime Minister, or that he created a prime ministerial system. The bases of his political system, namely the attempt to control as much patronage as possible and to retain the support both of king and Parliament, were far from new, though Walpole's determination to remain in the Commons rather than going to the Lords, as Harley and Stanhope had done, was an important development, reflecting his belief that the Commons were both more influential and harder to manage.

Public opinion

Another sphere in which Walpole did not innovate was that of the manipulation of public opinion. According to the findings of the Committee of Secrecy set up in 1742 to inquire into his misuse of public funds, Walpole spent over £50,000 on the production and distribution of newspapers and pamphlets in the 1730s. Large sums of public money were spent in London, on purchasing existing newspapers, establishing new ones and paying authors. Walpole also sponsored the production of pro-ministerial pamphlets. However, these activities were not new.

Although the patronage of the press by the Stanhope–Sunderland ministry is still a subject awaiting attention, it is clear that the Harley ministry developed many of the techniques that Walpole was to use. Furthermore, Walpole's interest in and concern about the press should not be exaggerated.[17]

The early eighteenth-century interest in the political possibilities of print reflected the concern shown by politicians about public opinion. However much politics might appear to be exclusively an occupation or hobby for the upper orders exercised at Court, in country houses and in Parliament, it is clear that this was not the case. In recent years historians have drawn attention to the often radical dimension of popular politics and suggested that it was of considerable importance. Attention has been devoted both to the electorate and to those who, though they did not possess the vote, could seek to influence political decisions. There were many boroughs with small electorates, such as Malmesbury with 13 voters, Gatton with 22 and Whitchurch with 85. In Cornwall 1400 voters elected 42 borough MPs. There were only 94 contests at the general election of 1741. The comparable figures for 1715, 1722 and 1727 were 119, 154, 114. Eighteenth-century election campaigns were expensive and generally financed by the candidates themselves, especially on the Opposition side. In large counties and boroughs they were often just too expensive to contest. In addition, in many of the small constituencies there was rarely an election. The Jacobite Earl of Orrery complained in 1721, 'there are so many little venal boroughs that 'tis to be apprehended a majority will hardly be carried by the inclinations of the people only'.[18] At the beginning of the century, when its electorate was about 800, the representation of Flintshire was shared by the heads of its leading Tory families, an agreement renewed in 1731. From 1747 the Mostyn family represented the county in every Parliament until 1837.

However, an absence of a contest did not mean that there was no element of representation. Most of the voters were deferential, but this did not mean that they simply responded to instructions. Borough patrons were expected to tend their constituency, dispensing patronage and defending its interests. A failure to do so could lead to the rejection of the patron's influence. William Stanhope, who had been elected for Derby in 1715, complained when not re-elected in 1722 while envoy in Spain. He wrote that his fate had been: 'when out of sight to have all services forgotten, for certainly I did for that town the greatest they had to wish for, by making their river navigable'.[19] In 1732 Sir Richard Grosvenor nearly lost his family's electoral interest in Chester, because of his opposition to a scheme to widen the River Dee in order to help the town's trade. Francis Whitworth, a ministerial candidate defeated at Minehead in 1722, complained, 'one would imagine there was a law made for bribery, and not against it'. His elder brother Charles won an uncontested seat at Newport, Isle of Wight, that year. Despite support from the governor of the Isle and the fact that the electorate numbered 24 only, the members of the corporation, the election cost Whitworth £700, although he was assured that 'as matters go, 'tis reckoned a cheap bargain'.

In the large boroughs and large counties there was a sizeable electorate, about 6000 in Norfolk, over 15,000 in Yorkshire, nearly 5000 in Bristol. These electorates were difficult to control, and the bitter contests in these seats were seen often as a comment upon the popular will and the popularity of the government, as in 1734 when MPs who had supported the Excise Bill were rejected by such constituencies as Bristol, Kent, Newcastle and Norfolk. In seats with large electorates there were often several important patrons and relations between them could be of crucial importance. In Sussex, where there were about 4000 voters in the county election, the dukes of Newcastle, Richmond and Somerset devoted considerable effort to influencing their dependants. In 1733, 'the Duke of Somerset at the entertainments this Xmas for the tenants and other freeholders under his Grace's influence has insisted on one vote for Mr. Pelham, and to reserve their other till farther orders'. In 1719 Newcastle claimed that he controlled 16 Commons' votes, most of which were of Sussex MPs.[20]

Had public opinion been restricted in its impact to the years in which elections were fought, then it would have made little impression on the political system. However, there were other methods by which the seemingly exclusive political system could be influenced by opinion 'out-of-doors'. Parliament and the ministry could be affected by organised extra-parliamentary pressure groups, by petitions and by nationwide instruction campaigns. The weak nature of the rather small government bureaucracy, and the widespread reliance of the ministry on outside bodies for advice, and even for assistance in the drafting of legislation, helped to increase the impact of lobbying groups.

Ministerial policy and parliamentary decisions were influenced greatly by mercantile pressure groups. The 1726 Act against importing foreign plate was drawn up by the Goldsmiths Company. The progress of the Anglo-Russian commercial negotiations in 1733–4 was affected by the Russia Company whose advice was sought by the ministry. Some mercantile groups, such as the East India Company, had very close links with the ministry.[21] Walpole's personal links with the directors of the major chartered trading companies and of the Bank of England were close, and helped to explain his sound grasp of financial matters and his ability to manage the government's fiscal interests. They also played a major role in enabling these groups to influence the ministry. Walpole also sought to influence London politics through his City friends,[22] and to increase their power within the metropolis. The City Elections Act of 1725 defined the freeman franchise as narrowly as possible and imposed an aldermanic veto on the actions of the more popular and Tory-inclined Common Council. Walpole's intention was clearly to limit the volatility and independence of popular London politics, and he sought to achieve his aim by means of legislative action and the definition of a favourable group through patronage and shared interests.[23] Other mercantile groups, such as the merchants trading to the West Indies, did not enjoy the same links with Walpole. However, their pressure-group tactics, a well-organised petitioning and propaganda campaign, were very successful in persuading Parliament to pass a series of measures in their favour, such as the Molasses Act of 1733 and the Sugar Act of 1739.[24] Nevertheless, it was a mistake to claim that Britain was 'governed by a parcel of merchants', or, as in 1718, that the Spanish trade was so essential that the ministry would not risk war with Spain. Mercantile lobbying was vociferous and left much documentary evidence but this has led to an exaggeration of its importance. Much of the lobbying was at cross-purposes. The *Evening Journal* in 1727 noted: 'The Turkey merchant writes against the East-India Company, the Woollen Manufacturer against the calicoes'. An examination of diplomatic records reveals that the ministry's commitment to the interests of trade was patchy. Relations with minor states could be greatly influenced by the issue. Complaints from the merchants and sugar refiners of Bristol in 1734 led to British pressure for a reversal of Venetian legislation affecting their interests. Moves in 1732–3 to restrict Hamburg efforts to benefit from the East India trade, and in 1734–5 to protect British trade from Danish attempts to blockade Hamburg, reflected pressure from British commercial interests.

However, with larger states, from whom Britain sought political advantage, the picture was very different. The 1720s and 1730s saw most European states passing protectionist legislation that harmed British trade. British diplomats were instructed to complain, and threats of parliamentary retaliation were made, but these complaints were subordinated to the need for good relations. This was certainly the case with Denmark, Sardinia and Sweden. Trade with Russia was sacrificed to political considerations in the 1710s and 1720s. Thus, the effectiveness of commercial lobbying, the openness of the political system to pressure 'out-of-doors' in this sphere, should not be exaggerated. It would have been unrealistic diplomatically to adopt commerce as a guiding principle. As Horatio Walpole pointed out in 1735: 'if a merchant of London, and of Amsterdam were to be the ministers of the political conduct to be observed between England and Holland, instead of preserving a union between the maritime powers, the two nations would be constantly in a war with one another.'[25]

The political impact of commercial pressure, accompanied by popular discontent, was seen in the War of Jenkins' Ear. Spanish attacks on British merchants in the West Indies, who, the Spaniards claimed, with a great deal of truth, sought illicitly to breach the Spanish commercial monopoly in their empire, had been a major parliamentary issue in the late 1720s. Its successful revival a decade later led to accusations of a supposed ministerial failure to defend vital British interests. Sustained pressure from mercantile groups and an Opposition press and parliamentary campaign had a significant impact. Horatio Walpole wrote in November 1737 of 'the clamour of the merchants' waking Newcastle up. Two months later the Spanish first minister, La Quadra, told the British envoy that the government 'ought not to take the noise and clamours of our [British] subjects for well-founded complaints'. The ministry negotiated a settlement with Spain – the Convention of the Pardo – and defended it successfully against virulent opposition attacks in the session of 1739, but when difficulties arose over the diplomatic settlement, their room for political manoeuvre was restricted drastically by the consequences of the domestic debate over policy.[26]

Commercial lobbies were matched by religious pressure groups.[27] The episcopacy enjoyed ready access to the corridors of power, and did not need to resort to extra-parliamentary campaigns.[28] Furthermore, the uneasy relationship between the predominantly Whig and pro-ministerial episcopacy, and the largely Tory parochial clergy, a relationship which had led to the prorogation in 1717 of convocation, the clerical Parliament, could not have encouraged the high clergy to instigate such campaigns.[29] The societies for the reformation of manners, institutions which indicated the strength and social awareness of Anglican piety, could have been used to exert pressure, but the episcopacy preferred to trust to their more reliable links with the Whig ministry. Such links did not preclude religious campaigns, such as that which Gibson mounted in the 1730s in his diocese of London, but they made them dependent on leadership from the top.

If the Church of England had operated in a different fashion it is possible that the explosion of popular piety associated with John Wesley and the Methodist movement he launched in the late 1730s could have been contained within the Church. John and Charles Wesley remained members of the Church of England all their lives and in 1756 the Methodist conference ended with a strong declaration by the Wesleys of their determination 'to live and die in the communion of the Church of England'. The ferment associated with Methodism, a tiny movement in the 1730s and 1740s but one that was to grow rapidly, indicated the strength of religious feeling among large sections of the community, particularly in the growing industrial communities and among the poor, groups unevenly served by the Church of England. Methodism rose to a certain extent on the ashes of Jacobitism, gaining support from much of the same constituency. The methods used by the Methodists – field preaching, itinerant lay preachers, and a cellular organisation based on the class, a group which met weekly – helped to channel their dynamism into an effective structure.[30] In eighteenth-century France, particularly in Paris, popular piety created major difficulties for the government.[31] Methodism did not present the same problems in Britain. Avoiding the radical implications of his preaching of the equality of all believers, John Wesley preached that the social hierarchy was divinely ordained. Autocratic by temperament, Wesley had no time for democracy. Possibly Methodism helped to secure the social, if not the religious, stability of eighteenth-century Britain. Methodism can be viewed as a substitute for revolution, promising Salvation and a personal assurance of grace as an escape from an engagement with this-worldly struggles. The major problem with such an analysis is that there is scant evidence, particularly for the first half of the century, that Britain was teetering on the brink of revolution, or that, if it was, Methodism was influential enough to prevent it. Despite, by modern standards, appalling social and economic inequalities and atrocious living conditions for a sizeable percentage of the population, revolutionary ideology was largely absent. The view that Methodism acted as a lightning conductor for the socio-economic strains present in society, and growing as a result of agrarian and industrial change, founders on the absence of indications of a widespread disenchantment with the system, and the absence of such indications can make talk of appalling conditions and inequalities appear anachronistic and heavily value-loaded.

Methodism did not operate as a lobby – Wesley having very few links with the Whig establishment and indeed, at one level, being in revolt against it – but the dissenting denominations sought to exploit their links with the Whigs. The Quakers, their activities co-ordinated by a permanent central committee, succeeded in securing amendments to legislation allowing them to affirm rather than to swear oaths, and in 1736 came close to obtaining a Tithe Act which would have removed the threat of prosecution for the non-payment of tithes. The Dissenters set up in 1727 a joint committee of ministers to concert pressure in favour of Indemnity Acts to allow them to hold office without taking the sacrament in the Church of England. Acts were passed accordingly in 1727–9, 1731 and 1733–43. They also established a lay organisation – the Dissenting Deputies – which sought to secure the repeal of the Test and Corporation Acts, and mounted major lobbying campaigns among parliamentarians in 1736 and 1739. They failed, Walpole warning the Commons that it must 'consider what was the opinion of people without doors, especially the Church'. Allegations that the Deputies were in Walpole's pocket have been refuted.[32] However, the Dissenters' success in achieving a serious parliamentary discussion of their interests reflected the openness of the political system to effective lobbying, as their achievement was disproportionate to their numerical strength. Walpole's willingness to support Indemnity Acts and to oppose the repeal of the Test and Corporation Acts was typical of the balancing conciliatory nature of his political art and also revealed much about his ecclesiastical policy. In 1751 his brother Horatio wrote:

> the late Lord Townshend and my Brother laid it down as a fundamental principle in their management of affairs . . . not to suffer any religious dispute to be canvassed in Parliament or any attempt to be made, if they could prevent it, being sensible that, however reasonable and conciliating any proposition might be to make a stricter union and harmony among all Protestants well affected to the Government, yet the high Church party that is disaffected is so numerous, and warm and ready to lay hold of any occasion to inflame the nation, that any alteration in the form of doctrine of the Church of England would be, although in itself desirable, and right, and perhaps trivial, a dangerous attempt, as productive of greater troubles, than the good expected from it could compensate.[33]

Most of the attempts to influence parliamentary conduct
related to legislation for private and local interests, such as
turnpike trusts. This reflected the fact that the bulk of parliamentary legislation and time was devoted to these interests, in
contrast to the twentieth century when Parliament is dominated
by the legislative programme of the government. As many local
interests were in competition (the town of Newcastle and
Sunderland over river improvements, for example), there was a
clear need to influence Parliament and much effort was devoted
to this end. Lobbying and the presentation of petitions were
frequent, with campaigning for these sectional interests related
often to the struggles of national politics. The same techniques
were used in the pursuit of political aims, largely by the
Opposition. Although the ministry was not averse to arranging
for suitable petitions and addresses to be presented, Walpole
never developed this in a systematic fashion. Possibly this
reflected a feeling that the Opposition used these methods more
successfully, and that it was, therefore, better to condemn the
attempt to dictate to Parliament, as ministerial spokesmen did,
than to seek to match the Opposition. Opposition spokesmen
stressed the need to heed opinion 'out-of-doors'. George Dodington warned the Commons in 1743 that if popular anti-Hanoverian-
ism was ignored the people would turn to Jacobitism:

> if every man in this House, were to be silent upon that head, the
> people without doors would soon find out what tools they were
> made of: they would soon perceive their being sacrificed to the
> interests and views of Hanover; and this would render every honest
> man in the nation not only discontented with our public measures,
> but disaffected to the illustrious family now upon our throne; the
> necessary consequence of which would be, that our present
> constitution must overturn our present establishment, or our
> present establishment must overturn our present constitution.

The following month the Earl of Sandwich called upon the Lords
to heed the general voice and oppose a continuation of subsidies
to Hanover:

> it may be hoped that these settlements will be adopted, and these
> resolutions formed by every man who hears, what is echoed

through the nation, that the British have been considered as subordinate to their own mercenaries . . . that foreign slaves were exalted above the freemen of Great Britain, even by the King of Great Britain, and that on all occasions, on which one nation could be preferred to the other, the preference was given to the darling Hanoverians.

In the same debate the Duke of Marlborough declared:

It is not possible to mention Hanover, or its inhabitants, in any public place, without putting the whole house into a flame, and hearing on every hand expressions of resentment, threats of revenge or clamours of detestation. Hanover is now become a name which cannot be mentioned without provoking rage and malignity, and interrupting the discourse by a digression of abhorrence.

Ministerial spokesmen disagreed with the idea of following opinion 'out-of-doors'. James, 13th Earl of Morton, a keen supporter of Walpole, agreed that the continuance of the Hanoverian subsidies was unpopular, but argued that, 'the man who would gain the people's favour by injuring their interest, is not a friend, but a sycophant'.[34]

This attitude, which was seen also in ministerial newspapers, such as the *Daily Gazetteer*, could be said to represent a Whig oligarchical distaste for public opinion.[35] It is equally probable that it reflected a decision to rely on a secure parliamentary majority and not to challenge the Opposition in the field of public opinion, upon which opponents were perforce obliged to concentrate. The result was that when the ministry was threatened with serious parliamentary difficulties, in 1730, 1733 and 1741–2, it suffered from its relative neglect of extra-parliamentary lobbying. Had Walpole in 1738–9 been able to orchestrate a campaign of petitions, addresses and instructions from groups or constituencies that feared the loss of their trade with Spain, or in 1733 in praise of the Excise scheme, his political, and in particular his parliamentary, position might have been eased. Such lobbying would not have been easy to achieve. Most of the trade with Old Spain (Spain itself as opposed to the Spanish empire) was controlled by Irish Catholics and Jews, groups of limited political importance in Britain.[36] However, there are few signs that Walpole made any effort to arrange such lobbying, in contrast with the petitions and Addresses in favour of North's American policy in 1775–6 and of Pitt's legislation in the 1790s.

The Opposition were far more active. All sorts of opportunities were used in order to disseminate their views. The Addresses from Opposition strongholds congratulating George II on his accession in 1727, many of which were printed in the newspapers, criticised ministerial policy, and pressed for the retention of Gibraltar, whose return the government was believed to be considering. Before parliamentary sessions during which they were hopeful of success, the Opposition mounted major propaganda campaigns, both to create a sympathetic climate of opinion among the political nation and to influence MPs. The first was done largely by means of the press. MPs were sent petitions for the redress of grievances accompanied by 'instructions' from their constituents, requesting them to vote in a particular way and to bring forward certain resolutions in Parliament. Particularly vigorous campaigns were mounted in 1733 and 1738–42. Walpole claimed, with some justice, that these campaigns were launched and organised by the Opposition, but it is also clear that they reflected a hostility to Walpole's policies that was not confined to the section of the political elite which constituted the Opposition. Much of the Opposition to the Excise Bill came from the towns and reflected not only the view of the merchants, but also of sections of the general population who demonstrated in London, parading wooden shoes, the symbols of supposed French slavery, and mobbing Walpole at the entrance to the Commons. London took a major role in organising Opposition activities in 1733 and 1738–42. The press, both ministerial and Opposition, was dominated by London, Scottish and provincial newspapers such as the *York Courant* and the *Newcastle Courant*, being composed largely of items from the London press. The press, therefore, served to spread knowledge of metropolitan developments, and to project the Opposition viewpoint throughout the country. London 'instructions' were copied in other constituencies, and in 1732 the *Craftsman*, after reporting the preparation of instructions in London, urged that this practice be emulated elsewhere. Some MPs took note of their constituents' views on political matters. In 1742 Andrew Mitchell, Under-Secretary for Scotland, argued that most of the MPs who voted for the repeal of the Septennial Act 'gave their assent only to please their constituents'. The same year the Tory MP Thomas Carew responded to a public letter from supporters in his Minehead constituency by sending an account of the political situation and his activities that was designed to be communicated to his 'good friends'.[37]

In 1728 Richard Buckner, the estate agent of the Duke of Richmond, wrote from Sussex to his master, then on holiday in Iberia:

> Politics is the only prevailing conversation at present, and there is no company, or set of men of what degree soever, who does not take upon them to decide matters as peremptorily as if they were at the bottom of the secret . . . They loudly complain of stagnation of trade, the capture of so many merchant ships, the dilatory proceedings of the Congress, and such general topics extracted from the *Craftsman* and *Fog*.

Eleven years later a medal criticising alleged British cravenness towards Spain circulated in Warwickshire, where it was claimed that 500 were sold. An Edinburgh commentator observed in 1742, 'At present every tailor here is turned politician'.[38]

Work on the 'popular' opposition to Walpole relies primarily on urban evidence. Recent studies on eighteenth-century towns have revealed that they were of great importance in the creation and definition of political attitudes.[39] However, the extent of their influence over the countryside is difficult to evaluate, particularly as most of the sources for popular political interest and participation, such as newspapers, are of urban origin. Clearly rural, like urban, interest and participation in national politics varied greatly. In 1715 Edward Southwell discerned little interest in the struggle between George I and the Jacobites and claimed that Somerset and Gloucestershire were, 'like to all Wales perfectly indolent which gets the better the King or the Rebels so as to toss Cross or Pile', presumably a reference to a popular game.[40] Struggles for local power and patronage, even if expressed in party terms, did not necessarily relate to or have

any links with national political struggles. Though numerous
urban areas, both large and small, lacked parliamentary representation in the eighteenth century, many of them, however, did
have a 'politics' of their own, so that corporation elections, not
to mention sundry local building projects, were often fiercely
contested. Studies of local politics and of elections do not
always reveal the dominance of national concerns. In 1733 John
Plumptre, soon to be elected MP for Nottingham, reported from
the city to the Duke of Newcastle: 'I do not hear that the Excise
Bill has made any great alteration, amongst the freeholders, one
way or another; except amongst such of them as are concerned
in trade, and such as were wavering from us and grumblers
before who now take a handle from it to justify a behaviour
which they had been much at a loss to give a reason to.' There
was no contest in 1734, the Tories and the Whigs each putting
up one candidate only, in order to save expense, an agreement
maintained in each general election from 1727 until Nottingham
was contested in 1754. In Hull national politics played little role
in local affairs. On the other hand, Cholmley Turner's 'former
actions' as MP, including his support for the Convention of the
Pardo (the attempt to settle differences with Spain in 1738),
the Septennial Act, the standing army and ministerial fiscal
demands, were mentioned or alluded to in public and private
attempts to elicit support for the Tory candidate in the Yorkshire
by-election in 1741. In 1744 Sir John Cust, pro-government MP
for Grantham, was informed by a Lincolnshire protégé: 'In the
neighbourhood your voting for the Hanoverians has been . . .
represented to ignorant people in very bad colours . . . no pains
have been spared to get aright, and it is pretty much so by this
time.'[41]

There is need for caution in extrapolating from the political
culture of print, with its starkly differentiated partisan positions,
to that of the localities. It is probable that historians, in
concentrating on the fashionable subject of urban studies, have
neglected the interests of the bulk of the population, and possible
that the stress on urban activities has led to an undervaluation
of rural conservatism. There is also the danger that in social and
cultural history disproportionate attention has been devoted to

urban developments. Most of the obvious manifestations of culture in the early eighteenth century – theatres, subscription concerts, reading rooms, libraries, bookshops, assembly rooms, the growth of the press – were urban, as were many of the schemes for social 'improvement' and/or control: poor relief, welfare provision, crime control and medical improvement. The extent to which rural society shared in their benefits is unclear. The pattern which has emerged from studies of education is suggestive: towns, especially market towns, advanced in the early eighteenth century while the village poor had few educational resources. By the late eighteenth century country education was generally much better, while the industrialising towns fell sharply back. The countryside was not cut off from the towns; the latter played a major role as markets for the countryside and as centres of and for consumption, whilst road links improved with the spread of turnpike trusts by the mid century. There was less overt competition between urban and rural industry than in many areas of Europe. It has been argued that the eighteenth century witnessed the development of a consumer society in Britain.[42] Pedlars from towns brought wares to the countryside; rural readers read newspapers, acquiring information about urban opinions, fashions and products. However, it is too easy to assume that rural society responded rapidly or evenly to urban developments, or that rural values and opinions were determined by those of the towns. The *Craftsman* might write of London in 1727 that, 'the eyes of the whole nation are constantly fixed on the conduct and proceedings of this city, as the Primum Mobile of Great Britain', but then the newspaper was printed there.

The electoral system favoured the urban voter disproportionately, particularly if he lived in a small borough. The 40 English counties, with an electorate of nearly 160,000, returned only 80 MPs, or one per 2000, whereas the 205 English boroughs, with an electorate of only 101,000, returned 409 MPs, or one for less than 250 voters. Towns with a population of over 10,000 were either under-represented or unrepresented. Political programmes were conceived and debated in London, the largest town, the seat of the Court and the centre of the legislature, executive and judiciary. The public discussion of policy, for example, the contrast between the respective weights in parliamentary and press discussions attached to 'Trade' and the 'Landed Interest' revealed the influence of urban norms, the political importance of the urban 'cash' economy as opposed to the landed 'wealth' economy. Trade dominated discussion of the economy, and of ministerial policy towards the economy, in an unbalanced fashion, and became a very potent political cause, as Walpole discovered to his cost in 1733 and 1738–9. The interests of trade and agriculture could not be separated completely, but the latter tended to lack the vocal advocates of the former. Thus, Walpole never received the political credit that he deserved for his pro-agrarian policies of the mid 1730s: the attempt to shift the burden of taxation away from the land tax, and British neutrality in the War of the Polish Succession, which permitted a boom in grain exports to the Mediterranean. The latter was of major benefit for the economy, in terms of specie gained for the nation and aid for the economy of the grain-producing areas. These were depressed as a result of slack domestic demand, caused by the stagnant demographic situation that characterised the age of Walpole, and of low prices caused by good harvests.[43] In comparison, the losses suffered when a few British merchantmen, most of whom had been smuggling, were seized by the Spaniards in the West Indies were minor, and yet it was these that received attention and became a potent political issue.

It is possible that the urban opposition to Walpole was unrepresentative, first of rural opinion, and secondly of feeling in the towns themselves. It is clear that the Excise Bill aroused widespread fears and that Spanish depredations created concern in a few ports, but it is not apparent that this amounted to a sustained, widely based hostility to the Walpole regime or to the policies of the ministry. In 1733, the Duke of Newcastle found unexpected opposition in Sussex:

> These gentlemen have been in several parts of the county in a
> body, inflaming the people with the cry of the excise, standing
> armies, and everything that will serve their turn . . . when I came
> into the Country, I found them universally against the excise,
> and that the clamours that had been raised upon it, and the sup-

posed consequences of it, had made an impression upon many individuals.

Nevertheless, he was convinced, with reason, that the ministerial candidates would succeed, and in 1739 he found Sussex 'in very good humour', noting 'hitherto the attempts of the enemy to work them up are unsuccessful'. In 1741, however, supporters of the ministerial candidate in the Yorkshire by-election claimed that the Opposition was using the Convention of the Pardo as 'a cant word, adopted without meaning, and echo'd out against the people to inflame and abuse them'.[44]

Many demonstrations of popular concern were episodic, linked to particular grievances that would have caused trouble whoever was in the ministry. This was true of riots based on the economic situation, such as food riots, or the Wiltshire weavers' disturbances, of the riots near Bristol against new turnpike roads in the mid 1730s, and of the Porteous riot in Edinburgh in 1736, a breakdown of law and order that stemmed from popular anger at a legal decision by the ministry. This did not prevent Opposition politicians, such as the Tory MP Sir William Wyndham in May 1737, from trying to make political capital out of riots. Thomas Hay, writing from Edinburgh in 1742, discerned expressions of discontent at different social levels:

> People here have been of late a little mobbish in different ways the better sort in sowing malicious clamour . . . we have sometimes little poetical satires or comical and satirical pamphlets . . . from London. . . . The lower sort of people sometimes deal in mobbing properly so called. . . . The practise of mobbing ought to be checked. It is not good to accustom the populace to do themselves justice. . . . The abominable practice of raising dead bodies the only cause of the late riots is very provoking which disposes people in general to have some compassion for such a mob as revenged themselves on the persons suspected and therefore upon these occasions matters must be conducted with prudence so as neither to overlook the thing altogether nor to punish the rioters over rigorously. . . . If the inferior magistrates takes good care to punish those villains . . . the populace will discontinue their mobbish practices.

Food riots, such as those in Cornwall in 1727–9 and 1737, North

Wales in 1727 and in many areas in 1740, were often against the export of grain from a region where prices were rising and shortages being created in part by the demand from wealthier areas. In 1715 Daniel Dering wrote: 'I have no notion that a crowd of peasants got together can make any resistance against standing regular forces.' However, the attempt to implement the Militia Act of 1757 in Bedfordshire revealed the weakness of the government when faced by a breakdown in law and order. The Lord Lieutenant, the Duke of Bedford, complained that: '59 men of the Royal Regiment of Horse Guards (which is all the force we have now amongst us) are not sufficient to defend the whole county from the insolence of a riotous rabble.'[45]

Demonstrations of an explicitly political nature were relatively uncommon, except for the semi-ritualised displays of party strength during the elections. The mass of the population may have been concerned about ministerial policy, though there is little evidence on this point, but they did not participate in the political process, either directly by means of voting, or indirectly, by means of extra-parliamentary activity. Some, particularly in the towns, who did not possess the vote, were nevertheless willing to attempt to influence the political process. Politics was not the preserve of an oligarchy or a simple matter of patronage. However, to argue that these largely urban elements reflected the whole of extra-parliamentary opinion is mistaken. Were it true it would be difficult to explain how the Whig oligarchy managed to survive, short of postulating some mistaken theory based on coercion. Rather one could suggest that critical opinion 'out-of-doors' represented the views of a minority, in short that the Whig oligarchy and its Opposition, however widely the latter is defined, were both minorities faced with the apathy, ignorance, poverty and lack of political commitment of the bulk of the population.

In contrast mid-century Methodism was a genuinely popular movement, in which a lot of poor people, such as the fishermen of Cornwall, or the Tyneside and Kingswood miners, joined, although there were also violent demonstrations against Wesley, especially when Methodists tried to stop popular activities. Patriotism, the political creed of the opposition Whigs, and

Toryism appear not to have enjoyed the popularity that Methodism was to inspire. Partly this was a matter of organisational technique; the field service and the itinerant preacher could reach more people and capture their attention and support more effectively than newspapers. Partly it was a matter of content. The evangelical intensity of Methodism, with its promise of a new birth in Jesus Christ, that would lead to a purer life on earth and heavenly reward thereafter, excited a fervour that was lacking from the Opposition's call for a moral purging and rearmament of the State by the banishing of the corrosive force of corruption and the reinstatement of true distinctions, such as merit and quality, good kingship and honest ministers. Bolingbroke's political programme, as advanced in the *Craftsman*, and *The Idea of a Patriot King*, might interest political thinkers, but it was too abstract and remote to command widespread support, and much of the population was illiterate anyway.

Walpole and his successors opposed Patriotism, not Methodism, which was a force to be reckoned with by Walpole's successors, rather than by Walpole himself. Had they, in concert with the Church of England, sought to contain Methodism by banning field preaching and the erection of chapels, a very dangerous situation would have arisen. No such attempt was made. The tolerant ecclesiastical policy followed by the Old Corps Whigs permitted the development of Methodism, a theologically orthodox but ecclesiastically disruptive force, without the latter threatening social or political stability. This was a considerable achievement, for charismatic, evangelical religious movements could, and indeed can, pose major problems for society and, if they fall foul of the political system, for the stability of the state. Much was due to Wesley's disinclination to see himself as a political figure. Wesley condemned placemen, rotten boroughs, press-gangs, and turnpikes, and in the 1730s could best be described as a Tory. However, politics was for him a distraction from his religious mission, and the absence of ministerial opposition to his mission encouraged his avoidance of political crusading. Wesley responded to allegations of Jacobitism in 1744–5 by producing his *Word to a Freeholder* (1747) in which he urged his followers to show their loyalty by voting for ministerial Whig candidates in the first general election after Walpole's fall.

Had the Patriot movement or the Tories enjoyed the popular support and emotional dynamic that Methodism was to inspire, they would have presented major threats to the Walpole ministry. That neither did so reflected the dominance of religious commitment in a society that was far from secular. Religion was of fundamental importance for ideological, social, political and cultural reasons; norms of conduct and concepts of legitimacy were based on religious ideas. A secular opposition movement therefore stood little chance of gaining widespread popular support for a campaign of political reform and change, unless the government should seek to implement major changes that would have an effect throughout the nation, something the ministry scarcely possessed the machinery to attempt. In the absence of such moves, opposition political movements were handicapped by their remoteness from the concerns of the bulk of the population and from movements for religious revival, such as the so-called 'Great Awakening' of the eighteenth century which affected Britain, America and Germany. This explains much about the weakness and lack of success of the opposition to Walpole, the Wilkite opposition of the 1760s, the reform movement of the late 1770s and early 1780s and the opposition to the younger Pitt in the 1790s. However much the Opposition might claim to be popular or to reflect the will of the people, neither claim was true. There was no possibility of mobilising a truly radical nationwide popular campaign to bring down the ministry and transform the political system, though the early months of 1780 might be an exception, or of popular resistance to overturn the Whig oligarchy, and the parliamentary Opposition did not wish to do either. When in 1742 Chesterfield reflected on 'popularity which I am convinced will always be against those who are in', he implied that an important distinction existed between dissatisfaction with government and support for a specific alternative.[46]

In the 1732 Commons debate over the ministerial proposal for a revival of the salt duty the Opposition Whig MP Edward Vernon described the bill as 'only to ease the rich at the expense of the poor', adding that 'ninety nine in a hundred of the people would not put up with the tax, and that he should expect, if he voted for it, to be treated like a polecat and knocked on the head'.[47] Such a method of enforcing the popular will had no influential supporters, and Opposition publicists had to be very careful about advocating extra-parliamentary agitation. If, as in November 1742, MPs from constituencies 'whence most violent instructions have been sent' voted in a contrary fashion[48] there was little that could be done to influence their conduct, although on the eve of an election the situation was different, as Walpole discovered to his cost over the Excise Scheme. The *Craftsman*, in its essay of 6 April 1728, presented the fictional history of the Kingdom of Timbutam in Persia, an allegory of British developments. In this account the rule of the chief minister lasted until royal intervention – 'till the complaints and cries of the people (which were now grown almost universal) reached the Court and pierced the ears of a most indulgent Prince.' Defending Addresses to the monarch, the *Craftsman* of 8 July 1727 claimed: 'The first design of this practice was manifestly to make the Prince regnant acquainted with the genuine sense, and opinions of his People.' In fact neither George I nor George II was willing to heed the 'cries of the people' or of politicians who argued that Walpole was unpopular. Bolingbroke, although successful in his effort to achieve a personal audience with George I in 1727, failed to persuade him to dismiss Walpole. The Earl of Stair's attempt in 1733 to influence Queen Caroline against Walpole likewise failed.[49]

The Patriots might claim to represent the people, but they did not wish to increase popular participation in politics and had no real interest in a reform of the electoral system. In part this demonstrated the gap between the 'political nation', centred in London, and the rest of the country. The former was greatly concerned about political questions and prepared to participate in extra-parliamentary action, the latter in general was not. The Opposition's failure to bridge this gap was arguably crucial to its fortunes and to the failure of 'Patriotism' as an eighteenth-century movement. However, such an assessment assumes a degree of unity for the Opposition that may be misleading.

Prominent politicians who wished to manoeuvre themselves into royal and ministerial favour had different objectives from those who had little or no hope of such favour.

Stability and strife

H. T. Dickinson has suggested recently that: 'political stability did not rest simply on the absence of strife, tension and disputes. It was also the product of a political system that was flexible enough to contain the competing demands of different interests and rival pressure groups.'[50] This is an important point that throws much light on the vexed question of stability. The fact that rival interest groups were willing and able to compete within the system was a source of stability as they did not need to seek to alter the framework. The openness of the parliamentary and government system to lobbying was very significant in this context, as was the fact that most lobbying came from those who possessed power, wealth and status and that these groups were well represented in Parliament and government. Furthermore, Dickinson's argument that strife was synonymous with stability raises the point that standards of tolerable strife could vary. To appreciate the latter it is necessary to realise that all states in this period possessed a political system that had to cope with disparate and often contrary demands from various pressure groups. In 1773 the French foreign minister told the British envoy: 'that he had an opposition to combat as well as our ministry, and that it should be reciprocally considered that everything could not be done that was desired.' In 1787 the Spanish prime minister, Count Floridablanca, told the British envoy in Madrid that though Carlos III of Spain: 'had not literally a House of Lords and Commons to satisfy, and a professed opposition to encounter, yet he had also a species of Parliament, a publick, and a discontented party to manage, and that it was not in his power to do in every respect what his inclination might dictate.' In 1733 Cardinal Fleury of France excused his policies by reference to the force of public opinion.[51]

In this respect the situation in Britain was similar to that in most of the Continent. The satisfaction of interest groups or the reconciliation of competing groups called for considerable political skills, more so in states, such as Britain, Sweden and the United Provinces, where active representative institutions and a relatively free press enabled the debate over policy to be more public and created additional problems of political management. Walpole possessed these skills and his employment of them played a large role in ensuring political stability during his ministry. He was able to accommodate most of the powerful interest groups in the country, pre-eminently so in the crucial ecclesiastical sphere, where Dissenters and the Church of England were, if not completely contented, at least not placed in a position where they could feel totally defeated. A broadside writer of 1745, allegedly publicising Walpole's will, felt able to suggest that the ex-minister had ordered the engraving on the box that was to contain his embalmed heart of the following lines from Pope's *Essay on man* (1733):

> For Forms of Government let fools contest,
> Whate'er is best administer'd, is best:
> For Modes of Faith let graceless zealots fight;
> His can't be wrong whose life is in the right:[52]

In the political sphere he was less accommodating. Tories did not enjoy many of the fruits of patronage. However, Walpole's policies owed much to Tory ideas, and it was possibly due in part to this, as well as to the unfavourable international situation and the experience of defeat, that Jacobitism was of relatively little importance between the Atterbury Plot and the deterioration of relations with France at the beginning of the 1740s. It was not that support for Jacobitism ceased to exist, but rather that most of the prominent Tories in England proved unwilling to participate actively in Jacobite intrigues in this period. Tories, such as the Earl of Orrery, sent discouraging reports to the Pretender, informing him that support for the Jacobite cause in England was weak, and that nothing could be done without the assistance of a foreign army.[53] The quiescence of the British Jacobites during the international crisis of 1725–31 and, in particular, on the accession of George II, suggests that the pro-Jacobite Tories did not see any opportunity for action, but also that the Tories were not driven by Walpole's policies to a position of desperation. A master of the art of the politically possible, Walpole understood the position of the Tories and acted accordingly.

Walpole and the alternatives

It is unclear whether any of the other politicians of the period could have governed with more success. Some were better informed on foreign affairs (Bolingbroke, Carteret, Chesterfield, Harrington), but none enjoyed Walpole's mastery of the arts of political management and of fiscal affairs, and few possessed his administrative competence and parliamentary skills. It is probable that other ministers would have pursued different policies. Some would have followed a more pugilistic foreign policy. Carteret, Pulteney, Harrington and Newcastle would probably have taken Britain into the War of the Polish Succession. Lacking any real interest in fiscal matters they would have been unlikely to have introduced the Excise Bill. Some, such as Newcastle, would have sought a Whig-only ministry, others, such as Carteret, would probably have been prepared to turn to the Tories had they been faced with a strong Opposition Whig grouping. Before his death, Carteret's patron, Sunderland, had moved in this direction. All would have sought to use Walpole's methods of patronage and parliamentary management, although, as most were in the Lords, the latter would have been more difficult. All the Whig alternatives to Walpole would have been accused of corruption, although Carteret, a patron of the arts and a friend of Swift, or Chesterfield might well have enjoyed a better literary reception than Walpole, at least to begin with. Possibly the Whigs would have fared less well without Walpole. None of the alternative leaders was as adept politically, and entry into the War of the Polish Succession, though possibly initially popular, might well have been disastrous.

On the other hand, Walpole endangered the ministerial position in the 1734 elections by his espousal of the Excise scheme, whilst the chances of success in the 1727 elections were increased for any ministry by the relative popularity of the new king and by his keen support of the Whigs. Had Walpole fallen earlier than 1742, for example in 1727 or in 1733 over the Excise, and been replaced by an alternative Whig ministry, as many thought likely, much would have depended on whether he would have been willing to lead an Opposition in Parliament, and whether, as seems unlikely, the Tories would have been prepared to co-operate with him. George II's support was crucial to Walpole in 1733, but George chose well. Walpole's unwillingness, other than in 1733 and 1736, to rock the boat by introducing contentious legislation may well have helped to produce an atrophy of the legislative process, always a danger in a political system unwilling to anger powerful interests and based on a complex and sensitive balancing act. However, his lack of enthusiasm for innovation reflected an awareness of the nature of the system. As the *Northampton Mercury*, a pro-ministerial newspaper, noted in 1723: 'The first safety of princes and states lies in avoiding all councils or designs of innovation, in ancient and established forms and laws, especially those concerning liberty and property and religion.'[54] This was also the first safety of ministers, and Walpole's longevity as first minister owed much to his realisation of this.

It is unfashionable today to ascribe much influence to individuals, but the continuation of the Walpole ministry, the political stability that this represented and fostered, and the peaceful economic, social and religious developments for which it provided a framework, or which at least it did not impede, owed much to Walpole's political skills. Writing in the centenary year of the Excise Bill Sir Robert Peel took exception to the view of Viscount Mahon, later Earl Stanhope: 'You have not made sufficient allowance for the difficulties with which he had to contend; you have not given him sufficient credit for the complete success with which he surmounted them; and you have attached too much weight to the accusations which party rancour and disappointment preferred against him.'

Peel went on to give his opinion. He noted one of the keys to Walpole's success in Parliament, his charm – 'he first convinced, and then dined with them' and wrote:

Of what public man can it be said with any assurance of certainty, that, placed in the situation of Walpole, he would in the course of an administration of twenty years have committed so few errors, and would have left at the close of it the House of Hanover in equal security, and the finances in equal order? – that he would have secured to England more of the blessings of peace, or would have defeated the machinations of internal enemies with less of vindictive security, or fewer encroachments on the liberty of the subject?[55]

4

PARTY AND POLITICS UNDER THE FIRST TWO GEORGES

The classification of political groups is far from easy. Eighteenth-century political parties tended to lack an identifiable national leadership, an organised constituent membership and a recognised corpus of policy and principle around which to cohere and which could serve to link local activists to national activity. However, many modern political parties can only be described as coalitions; they are monolithic neither in organisation nor in policy. This test might be failed by modern parties in France, India, Italy and the United States. Some scholars are unhappy about the applicability of a two-party system at the constituency level, arguing that although Whig and Tory alignments did exist under those names in many constituencies, these feuds were often traditional and that family interest was paramount.[1] It is difficult to generalise on the relationship between electoral and parliamentary politics. The links between political behaviour in the localities and at Westminster varied widely, both over time and with reference to the type and size of constituency. There could be hostility to outsiders. In 1737 Viscount Lonsdale wrote to the Bishop of Carlisle about a local seat: 'I am very glad the Cumberland Gentlemen have agreed in uniting their interests, I hope it will prove a means of keeping out a stranger at Cockermouth.' Three years later their correspondence revealed the importance of local arrangements between prominent aristo-crats, Lonsdale writing: 'I received the honour of your Lordship's letter of the 15th wherein you are pleased to acquaint me that you had a message from my Lord Carlisle . . . which was that he would give no opposition to the present representatives for the county of Cumberland, if I gave none to those two who now serve for the City of Carlisle.' Lonsdale had 'no difficulty of saying that I will give no opposition to the present members'. A Whig–Tory division existed in Glamorgan that bore little relation to the behaviour of the participants in national politics. The representation of the Flint Boroughs was affected by a struggle for control between the Tory county gentry and George Wynne who gained control of the borough machinery, using it to create non-resident freemen. As Constable of Flint Castle he was able to nominate the returning officers and in 1734 they disallowed enough of his opponent's votes to give victory to Wynne, whose election was confirmed on petition by the government's majority in the Commons. Partisan Commons' voting on petitions and the disposal of crucial local posts were obvious examples of the importance of parliamentary politics for those involved in local conflicts. In 1741 the returning officers put Wynne at the head of the poll but he was unseated on petition in March 1742 by the anti-Walpole majority of the Commons. However, that was the last contest for several decades. After the death of the MP in 1753 a meeting of the local gentry unanimously adopted Sir John Glynne who wrote: 'As this county hath enjoyed great peace and tranquility for these many years in regard to the choice of its representatives, it hath been thought nothing could more contribute to a continuance of it than the nomination of some person to represent the borough who is most likely without any party prejudices to be agreeable to the several persons interested in this election.'[2] Clearly not all constituencies were dominated by two-party politics, and in some divisions within one of the parties were paramount. However, this is equally true of modern British politics. In many constituencies the major political battles are not those between Labour and Conservative, but most commentators agree that national politics, parliamentary debates and the struggles in many constituencies are dominated by this division. In general in the eighteenth century it was easier to resolve divisions within parties, by means, for example, of the pact between two leading Berkshire Tories to divide the future representation of the county, whereas differences between the parties were more intractable.

Part of the problem in the case of the eighteenth century is that far too little work has been done on local politics, with the conspicuous exception of London. There are a number of interesting theses on this subject,[3] but there is much still to be done. The nature of eighteenth-century local politics is important, not least because it provided the context for national and parliamentary politics. Much work on the latter has neglected the local context, but this approach appears increasingly inappropriate. The role of Parliament as an arbiter of local interests, or rather a sphere in which they competed, can be perceived, and the extent to which local government and politics were distinct and independent may be less than has been believed hitherto. Lionel Glassey has recently drawn attention to the manner in which agencies of central government:

> had established a presence in the localities, and helped to maintain and strengthen the links between Whitehall and the localities in their different ways in the early eighteenth century. The concepts of gentry 'autonomy' in the government of the counties, and of an oligarchical independence in the government of the towns, are firmly entrenched, but perhaps they need modification in certain respects. Those charged with the duties of local government not infrequently sought advice and direction from the centre. . . . Complete independence from the centre seems not even to have been desired, let alone achieved.

Struggles in London affected local patronage, James Lowther writing in August 1743: 'Mr. Pelham is now made first Lord Commissioner of the Treasury in opposition to those that wanted to bring in Lord Carlisle to court, so that places in Cumberland will go better than they have of late.'[4] The Howards, Earls of Carlisle, were like the Lowthers a significant factor in Cumbrian politics.

Given such links and the importance of Parliament and the government in affecting life in the localities in a wide range of matters, from the rate of taxation to the composition of the Bench, from the position of Dissenters to turnpike legislation, it is scarcely surprising that national politics had a local dimension.

Some scholars have sought to distinguish family interests and traditional feuds from party political behaviour, but this is not a very helpful distinction. Eighteenth-century parties lacked the institutional organisation of their modern counterparts. Instead, in many of the localities they were essentially organised in terms of family interests, a feature that is still the case in some parts of the world today. 'My Lord's Speedy Influence to his Tenants whom to vote for', was a form of political behaviour that in no way destroys the validity of a party description. John Clavering expressed the hope in Yorkshire in 1722 that the foundation of country assemblies for social purposes 'will have a good effect in making all parties live well together in the country and entirely banish politics which (in the country) breaks all good neighbourhood'.[5] However, three years later in Bath the visitors were divided into a Whig group led by the Duke of Richmond and a Tory one led by the Duke of Norfolk which had little to do with each other.

At the level of national politics several historians have denied the existence of a Tory party during the reigns of George I and George II.[6] Thomas's unhappiness with Colley's equation of the terms 'country gentlemen', 'the Country Party' and 'independents' with Tory partisanship is reasonable, but he goes too far in arguing that contemporary references by individuals to themselves as Tories do not contribute to the view that there was a Tory party. While to call an individual MP a Tory does not necessarily indicate his association with others, the use of 'Tories' as a collective noun clearly does, and such use was ubiquitous. The distinction between Opposition Whigs and Tories was made in some division lists. The sole archival reference Thomas cites comes from Sir Roger Newdigate's treatises on party. Writing in 1762 Newdigate denied the existence of a Tory party over the previous half-century.[7] Newdigate, however, was writing in a long tradition of Tories who denied the importance of party distinctions. From the 1720s Bolingbroke, Wyndham and other Tories who did want office had been deploying an anti-party rhetoric in order both to counter Walpole's Jacobite smear tactics and to elicit support at Court and among disaffected Whigs. Theirs was generally a call that party distinctions should and could be obliterated, rather than a declaration that they already had been. One opposition pamphleteer claimed in 1734 that 'Whig and Tory are only mere names'. In 1735 the *Daily Gazetteer*, a government-subsidised newspaper, claimed that, 'The Tories, or Craftsmen, for they are all one, have for some years endeavour'd to disguise themselves with the mask of Whigs'.[8]

Other commentators, such as Jacobites and foreign diplomats, were quite willing to refer to the existence of a Tory party.[9] Furthermore, Newdigate was a Tory not only 'by all modern reckoning', but also in the eyes of most contemporaries. The Whig Sir Charles Hanbury-Williams reported in 1747:

> the county of Middlesex has chose two Whigs by a majority of a thousand that never sent a Whig to Parliament before since the Revolution. And the reason they gave was that the two Whigs had subscribed money in the late Rebellion to defend their country while Sir Roger Newdigate (the first Tory candidate) was heading a Grand Jury who wanted but one vote, to find and present all associations and meetings for associations for the Defence of the Government as riotous assemblys and contrary to law.[10]

To argue, as a number of scholars have done, that the crucial parliamentary division was one of administration and opposition, makes little sense in terms of the period beginning in 1714. A crucial division existed between Tories and Opposition Whigs. This was made readily apparent after the Whig split of 1717. Walpole failed to use the Tories either to create an effective Opposition coalition that would override past differences or to force himself back into office. This prefigured the Bolingbroke–Pulteney 'country' campaign, a scheme which was as unoriginal as it was unsuccessful. The Tories and the Opposition Whigs were divided in 1718 over foreign policy and ecclesiastical issues, just as the Tories and the government Whigs were. The Tories pressed George, Prince of Wales, to vote against the Mutiny Act in the Lords but he refused to do so. Similar divisions pertained in the 1730s. Furthermore, Jacobitism was an issue that divided the Opposition. The situation in many of the constituencies matched that in Westminster. It proved very difficult to obtain adequate co-operation either between Tories and Opposition Whigs or between Tories and ministerial Whigs. It was impossible in the late 1710s and 1720s to devise suitable terms upon which all or most of the Tory party could join the ministry, though individual Tories, such as Harcourt and Trevor, were accommodated, at the price of abandoning their colleagues and principles. 'Agreeable to his last discourse with Mr. Walpole', Harcourt was added to the Privy Council in 1722, Newcastle noting: 'He has promised to be with us in every thing, and says the Tory party must be conquered. He comes in entirely to support the King and Whig Interest, and if he does not perform his promise he must expect no favour from the King.'[11] Trevor became Lord Privy Seal in 1726.

In late 1717 exploratory conversations took place between members of the ministry and some of the leading Tories, although there are no signs that anything more than an attempt to recruit one or two prominent Tories was seriously envisaged. Lord Trevor appears to have asked for places for more Tories than the ministry was willing to countenance. He demanded that the ministry discard its schemes for alleviating the legal position of the Dissenters. When George I received Trevor he was made to listen to a defence of the Utrecht settlement, hardly the way to endear the Tories to the king.[12] In 1723 Atterbury claimed that: 'he was offered the Bishopric of Winchester . . . by my Lord Sunderland, but that neither he nor Lord Trevor would engage till they saw the Church and army new modelled.' This the ministry was unwilling to do, and its decision was a wise one. The Tories were too divided to negotiate with satisfactorily. Trevor himself could carry few supporters. Furthermore, an alliance with all, or some, of the Tories was incompatible with the aims of the ministry. The Duke of Chandos, who sought a mixed ministry, explained to Harcourt in January 1718 that he had turned down the offer of a post, because it would be foolish to come into office alone: 'whereas were the assurances which were given me, and which I had authority to give your Lordship, punctually performed, viz. of the Act of Grace and of enlarging the bottom by taking in your Lordship etc. we could undertake to carry on the King's service in spite of all opposition, and by joining with the present ministers effectually support them from the rage of their enemies.'[13]

In September 1718 Bishop Gibson claimed that the Tories: 'will not come in at all unless they may come in, in a body. Depend upon it . . . that the Tories who call themselves the most moderate, will never break with the most rigid in order to incorporate with the Whigs: much less will any of them either moderate or rigid, be content to act in subordination to the Whigs.'[14] That subordination, however, was the sole basis upon which most Whigs were willing to deal with Tories. In 1723 the Duke of Newcastle observed: 'All sort of negotiations with the Tories is so dangerous as well as so useless.' In the same letter he noted that not all ministerial figures adopted this attitude. Newcastle did this by making a reference to links between the Tories and Lord Carteret, the Secretary of State for the Southern Department, whom Newcastle was to succeed the following year. However, Newcastle also observed that Carteret had broken off with the Tories 'thinking to carry his point with the Whigs, which he knows agreeable to the King'.[15]

Newcastle's letter draws attention to George I. Indeed, one of the surprising aspects of much discussion of the party question in the period 1714–60 is the failure to devote sufficient attention to the position of the monarch. Colley closes the second section of her study of the Tories with the observation that: 'their proscription was not irreversible. Always available, to distract from and enervate Tory popularism, was the prospect of a Tory return to power by high-political or parliamentary manoeuvre, which would preclude a more extensive and possibly subversive assault on the political and social order.' Earlier in the book Colley claims that George I and George II were very attracted by the idea of a mixed ministry: 'George I in 1717, 1721 and 1725, and his son in 1727, 1744 and 1746 (and these are only the instances for which we possess definite evidence) not only considered such a political solution but also went some way towards exploring its practicality.'[16]

This argument has been criticised. Reed Browning drew attention to what he termed 'the analytical confusion that underlies Colley's thesis' by juxtaposing her argument summarised above with her contention that 'Proscription preserved the Tory party's identity'. Browning noted Colley's claim that this exclusion distinguished them from country Whiggery. He could have added her statement that 'since all Tories were compelled into an opposition stance, the dichotomy between the party's Court and Country wings was normally obscured'.[17] Thus for Colley proscription explains both separate identity and internal cohesion, while the prospect of its end accounts for loyalty and participation in the established political process. However, not all scholars are impressed by her argument that George I and his son sought a mixed ministry.[18] Her evidence is scanty and by concentrating on Tory rumours she fails to devote sufficient attention to the high-political context of the episodes she discusses. In addition, Colley does not examine seriously the views of George I and George II. The scanty nature of the sources makes this far from easy, but critics might suggest that the available material has not been assessed adequately. In discussing the proposed admission of a larger number of Tories to the Commissions of the Peace in 1727, Colley cites George II's instruction to the Lord Chancellor, Lord King, to increase the number of Tories, but she ignores his injunction to 'still keep a majority of those who were known to be most firmly in his interest'. George ordered Lord King to keep that part of his instruction secret, which suggests that he was really seeking to curry popularity or to distinguish between Hanoverian and Jacobite Tories. Colley presents George II as 'fundamentally indolent', and therefore led by Walpole. It might be more appropriate to query her claim that the monarch sought a mixed ministry.[19] It is, however, fair to note that Colley does not subscribe to the strange notion that George I was able to enjoy a stable mixed ministry.[20] In 1721 it was George I who stopped Sunderland taking in the Tories. For Walpole, both in George I's last years and in 1727, the principal threat was posed not by Tories but by alternative ministerial figures, in George I's last years opponents within the ministry, and in 1727 young Whig aristocrats favoured by George II as Prince of Wales. Walpole was arguably more afraid of George II appointing Chesterfield

Secretary of State than of the possibility of his raising a Tory such as Sir Thomas Hanmer to the peerage.

This tension within the Whig elite has arguably received insufficient attention, because historians have been most concerned with parliamentary politics and especially those of the House of Commons. Paul Langford's study of the Excise crisis includes an important assessment of the crisis at the Court, but far too little is known about Court politics during the reigns of the first two Georges. The nature of the sources again poses a serious problem. As a result Hatton's biography of George I is better for his personality and foreign policy than for his attitudes towards and role in British politics. Daniel Baugh expressed scepticism on a number of counts with Hatton's arguments and commented: 'In the political sphere, George I's marked preference for conversations over memoranda and his strong desire to keep deliberations within a tight circle make the assessment of his role difficult. . . . Because of the nature of the evidence Hatton's argument respecting the King's political role rests largely on inferences.'[21]

Thus the court context of elite politics is obscure, the relationship between monarchs and leading politicians uncertain. If one of the principal purposes of organised political activity was to gain and retain office then it is clear that discussion of the nature of this organisation must include consideration of the relationship with the Crown and, in particular, the monarch's perception of the purposes for which aspirants sought office. This perception is the crucial point in any discussion of Tory Jacobitism. Ian Christie has proposed the acid test: 'is X a man with whom in a tight corner I should be happy to stand back to back, sure that he will defend my rear to the last and not turn and shoot me from behind.'[22] Those who would deny Tory Jacobitism have not provided any satisfactory suggestion as to how George I and George II were convinced or could be convinced that the Tories were loyal. This is especially important for the period 1714–27, the reign of George I and the accession of his son, during which Whig ascendancy was established. The conduct of many prominent Tories in this period was scarcely conducive to any argument that the Tory party, whose attitude could only be gauged by that of its leaders, should be trusted by the monarchy. It is probable that for George I and George II an indication as to the politician's possible attitude to Jacobitism was his actual record of votes and speeches on Hanoverian matters, though the scanty nature of the rulers' surviving correspondence must induce some caution on this point. On such a basis certain Whigs were not sound, but the majority of those who were unreliable were Tories.

Although the Tory ministry in the last years of Anne's reign had created a French alliance that could be seen as a prefiguration of the Anglo-French alliance negotiated by Stanhope in 1716, there were substantial differences between Tory foreign policy in 1713–14 and Whig policy several years later. Having betrayed Britain's allies, including Austria, Hanover and the United Provinces, at Utrecht, the Tory leaders after 1714, especially Bolingbroke, were adaptable enough to have been willing to support different alliances, but foreign policy divided them from the ministry for two reasons. The legacy of Utrecht was an important factor, skilfully presented by Whig propaganda, such as John Toland's *State Anatomy of Great Britain*, which described the Tories as 'men that pretend themselves the only Churchmen, and yet sacrifice the Protestant Interest everywhere'. More significant probably was the fact that, shorn of Bolingbroke's eager diplomacy and of the exigencies of office, many Tories had reverted to the 'Country' policy of opposing an interventionist role in European politics; or what Sunderland called 'the old Tory notion that England can subsist by itself'. However loyal or disloyal the Tories were to the house of Hanover, most were stridently anti-Hanoverian in proclaiming their support for a 'British' as opposed to a 'Hanoverian' foreign policy. In the Lords in 1718 Trevor 'spoke with great vehemence against' the Mutiny Bill and 'brought all the popular arguments against a standing army in time of peace'.[23]

Much of the argument against there being meaningful party divisions hinges on the question of whether the Whig–Tory conflict of Anne's reign should be seen as an anomaly or as the norm of political life in the first half of the century. Claims that the Hanoverian succession was followed by the eclipse of the Tories as serious contenders for office and the initial split and gradual disintegration of the dominant Whig party exaggerate Whig cohesion in the 1700s and ignore Walpole's success in the early 1720s in creating an effective political system. Some of those Whigs who were excluded or unhappy with their share of influence tended to oppose the ministry in Parliament, but it is possible to make too much of a basic alignment of Administration and Opposition. Many Whigs who fell out with the ministry did not oppose it in Parliament. The politics of the period cannot be understood if attention is devoted to Parliament alone, especially if the importance of the House of Lords is overlooked, as is so often the case. Any such concentration appears misplaced if it distracts attention from court and ministerial politics. This is especially true of one of the more neglected periods of eighteenth-century British history, the early 1720s and also of the last years of that decade. The parliamentary session of 1730 was difficult for Walpole and has justifiably received much attention. However, the ministerial/court crisis of that year was also extremely important. In British politics the most important developments in the period 1727–31 were the accession of George II, his decision to retain most of his father's ministers, the development of a working relationship between king and ministers, and the causes and consequences of the resignation of Townshend. Compared to these events, the activities, inside and outside Parliament, of the Opposition, however defined and described, were of less importance. Langford has indicated the role of court politics in 1733.[24] They also featured in the fall of Walpole. This could be presented in terms of the consequences for an increasingly divided ministry of having a divided court, the 1741 elections enabling the position of the Prince of Wales and a number of other dissatisfied figures to become more immediately crucial. The Whig reshuffle of 1742 was comparable to that of 1720. Court divisions and realignments were as important for the political disputes of the late 1710s and late 1730s–early 1740s as for the relative ministerial stability of the 1720s and early 1730s. Had Frederick, Prince of Wales, been older in 1730 and 1733 the political crises of those years might well have been very different. If it is possible to write a high-political history of early eighteenth-century Britain around the Court, it would be misleading to do so, if this led to the neglect of other spheres and causes of political activity. However, it would be no more misleading than to write the history around Parliament and parliamentary majorities. At one level Parliament was primarily a sphere for political disputes that originated elsewhere. However, Parliament became a crucial focus for the waging of these disputes and no alternative structure to Parliament developed. Christopher Wyvill's attempt to found one in 1779–80 failed, as did radical projects for 'Conventions' in the 1790s. There was a desire to work within Parliament, rather than an alienation from it. One sure sign of an incipient revolution or transfer of power is rightly held to be the slipping away of authority from the established institutions of state, to new, *ad hoc* unofficial bodies. Few societies have shown fewer symptoms of that than eighteenth-century England, and the Thirteen Colonies in North America offer an obvious contrast.

The relative importance of court politics is linked to the question of how far England can be described as an *ancien régime* state. It is certainly possible to demonstrate differences between England and particular European states in, for example, the size of the capital city and the role of towns and of international trade. Equally it is possible to suggest similarities. England was not alone in having to define relationships with a new dynasty with a German homeland, or with subordinate European territories, such as Scotland and Ireland. Local government in England, self-government by the social elite, and the consequent primary political problem, persuading the elite to govern in the interests of the centre, would have been all too familiar to many continental monarchs. The term *ancien régime* is misleading if it is taken to denote a uniform situation and consistent change. However, if the diversity that characterised continental circumstances and developments is appreciated, then England can be more easily comprehended as a country which, like all others, had both unique and comparable features and developments.[25]

If the role of the monarch and Court provides one element of continuity, what continuity existed in the field of political organisation? In an important essay David Hayton has argued that for the period 1689–1720 'Court and Country' are less appropriate for any model of political structure than Whig and Tory.[26] His conclusion could certainly be extended chronologically. Nevertheless, an element of discontinuity appears in mid century. Clark argued that his study of 1754–7: 'revealed in its necessary detail the crucial part of that tactical process by which the party system of the early eighteenth century disintegrated. In those years, the Tories were drawn into a Whig dogfight and deeply compromised; the Whigs were riven by personally-inspired conflicts for power within a ministry which was still formed on the basis of their party unity.'[27] Such developments were scarcely peculiar to this period. More significant was the process of seeking to conciliate and comprehend opponents within ministerial ranks, a marked tendency in the period that began with the fall of Walpole and, indeed, an inspiration that helped to precipitate his fall. The prime beneficiaries, as in the late 1710s and early 1720s, were dissident Whigs and Tories prepared to renounce their party, but the instability and realignments of the 1740s prepared the ground for those of the following decade. After the crushing defeat of Bonnie Prince Charlie at Culloden in 1746, Jacobitism was less of an option for the Tories and so had less influence on the perception of them by both the Whigs and George II. In the 1750s Tory cohesion and identity were seriously compromised.[28] If proscription and what lay behind it were a key to political activity in this period, then expectations concerning the future behaviour of Frederick, Prince of Wales, and George III, along with the actual behaviour of the latter, were clearly important. These helped to give a temporary air to the political arrangements of the late 1740s and late 1750s and to compromise any suggestion that Administration and Opposition were likely to be fixed.

A theory of political organisation for this period has to comprehend two essentially different political worlds, the fundamentally two-party alignment of the first half of the century, and the loose and shifting situation of the 1760s. A mid-century discontinuity is therefore indicated, centring on the years 1746–62. Events in the last fifteen years of George II's reign were clearly important, especially the effective demise of Jacobitism as a viable option, the consequent changes in the views of many Tories and the regrouping of Opposition politicians around Frederick, Prince of Wales, and the developments that followed his death in 1751. Newcastle and Pitt both wooed Tory support, while in certain constituencies in the 1750s a process of compromise was under way, Whig candidates seeking Tory support while Tory counterparts were deemed acceptable if they declared loyalty to the Hanoverians and 'a general adherence to the government'.[29] The policies of Frederick's eldest son, George III (1760–1820) were also important. George was determined to assert his independence from his grandfather's ministers. His views on foreign policy and his advancement of his favourite adviser, the Earl of Bute, led to clashes with Newcastle and Pitt who had co-operated in directing the ministry since 1757. Pitt resigned in 1761, Newcastle the following year, and Bute was appointed a Secretary of State in 1761 and then First Lord of the Treasury in May 1762.

Bute's rise aroused outrage and provided the occasion for much anti-Scottish propaganda. The 4th Duke of Devonshire, one of the leading Old Corps Whigs who held both a seat in the inner Cabinet and a major post at Court as Lord Chamberlain, claimed in November 1760: 'that a King of England, if he attempted to govern by a Favourite, would be unhappy for his affairs would always go ill, unless he placed his confidence in those whose abilities and situation rendered them the most considerable.' He was prepared to be blunt on the point both to George III and to Bute,[30] and it is clear from Devonshire's memoranda that one of the major bases of Old Corps Whig political activity was a belief in their own indispensability. Bute was disliked as an outsider and a royal favourite without political weight. Accustomed to view themselves as the natural advisers of the monarch, the Old Corps Whigs were unprepared to cope with the change from the elderly and exhausted George II to the more vigorous and unpredictable George III.

However, although George III's freedom of manoeuvre was restricted by war, as his grandfather's had been in 1744 and 1746, George III was able to dispense with the Old Corps and turn to his favourite, whereas George II had failed to keep Carteret in office against the opposition of the Old Corps led by Newcastle and Henry Pelham. By 1760 the Old Corps were suffering seriously from poor leadership. Pelham was dead, Hardwicke and Newcastle old and tired and the new generation of leaders weak and unimpressive. George III also benefited from war-weariness, from the natural support for a new monarch and from the influence and power that the Crown possessed which could be considerable if energetically and capably directed. George III's determination to exert his power disorientated the Old Corps Whigs who were used to a relationship between Crown and ministry in which royal initiatives were limited.

The combination of political changes that had been in process for about fifteen years and the actions of George III destroyed the old party system. In December 1761 the newly-elected Bamber Gascoyne told the Commons that there was 'faction in the ministry': Whig and Tory had been destroyed, but *personal* parties substituted in their stead'.[31] The Tories atomised, joining a variety of political groups, including the government establishment in the Commons. For at least the early decades of George III's reign, Commons' support for the government rested not on a party but on a coalition of first, the 'party of the crown, comprising Members of the Commons whose primary interest lay in public or court service, and whose overriding loyalties were to the sovereign and to the principle that the King's government must be carried on'; secondly, groups of active politicians seeking power each with their own followers; and thirdly, independent MPs essentially concerned with local interests but willing to offer loyal, though not uncritical, support. Opposition was comprised of critical independents and of groups of excluded politicians. There was also a 'party of the Crown' in the Lords. This analysis appears to be accurate for the 1760s, 1770s and 1780s. 'The apparent solidarity of the political line-up in the 1770s' for or against the policy of maintaining the integrity of Britain's North American empire by force 'merely cloaked, it did not supersede, the presence of personal groups'.[32]

The role of competing personal groups, operating without the semi-imperatives of fear and loyalty created by the Jacobite challenge and the response to it, helped to produce ministerial and parliamentary insecurity in the 1760s as George III struggled to find a ministry that he could trust and co-operate with and that could wield an effective majority in the Commons. The situation was aggravated by some disquiet as to how the constitution must now be viewed and by fears of rapid constitutional change towards royal tyranny or aristocratic oligarchy. The decade also witnessed an increase in extra-parliamentary political activity associated, in particular, with the favourable response in London to the maverick and charismatic John Wilkes in his challenges to the authority of George III's ministers and to Parliament.[33] However, there was no comparison between the actual and potential extra-parliamentary action that George I and George II's ministries had to consider and that which was faced in the period 1760–90. It was not until indigenous support for the cause of radicalism and for the example of the French Revolution developed in the early 1790s that a challenge similar to that posed by Jacobitism had to be confronted. The British supporters of the American rebels in the 1770s sought to alter the purpose of George III's government rather than the identity of the ruling dynasty or the nature of the constitution. Most extra-parliamentary action was really a matter of peaceful lobbying. In 1762 William Mure, a Scottish MP and adviser of Bute, who supported the agitation for Scotland to have a militia, as England did, wrote from Edinburgh to his friend Gilbert Elliot:

> . . . our Militia Meeting here. I joined them, both as a wellwisher to the cause, and to endeavour to prevent any unbecoming violence in their proceedings; or their improperly taking upon them to prescribe to their representatives by directing them the particular clauses of the Bill that should be passed. In both these I have succeeded. The whole that has been done is . . . sending a circular letter, very temperate, to every county and borough recommending to them to apply *in general* to their Members, for such a Militia as to the Wisdom of the Legislature might seem expedient.

The period 1760–90 was essentially politically stable. This may help to explain the ministerial instability of the 1760s. A series of short-lived ministries, those of Bute (1762–3), George

Grenville (1763–5), the Marquis of Rockingham (1765–6), William Pitt as Earl of Chatham (1766–8), and the Duke of Grafton (1768–70), succeeded one another until with Lord North, First Lord of the Treasury 1770–82, George III found a minister whom he could trust and who could manage Parliament, government and elections successfully.[34] As in the case of Walpole and Pelham before him and the younger Pitt subsequently, North both chose to lead the ministry from the Commons and was an expert on government finances. Like Walpole, North's fall was linked to the prosecution of an unsuccessful war. However, North's achievement in managing the Commons easily in sessions such as that of 1773, and his success in the 1774 general election reveal that the basis for ministerial and parliamentary stability had not been lost since the fall of Walpole and the death of Pelham. Parliamentary monarchy was still an effective system. It was to be proved so again during the ministry of Pitt the Younger both during the stable period of 1784–90 and during the subsequent years when Britain and its propertied elite faced domestic radicalism and a powerful France.

5

THE BRITISH DIMENSION

Walpole's world was still affected by the aftershock of earlier events. The 'Glorious Revolution' of 1688 and the consequent Jacobite challenge influenced English politics and government greatly, not least because of the effects of the two expensive and lengthy wars with France (1689–97, 1702–13) that were due substantially to William III's determination to limit French influence in western Europe. The effect of 1688 on Scotland and Ireland was more direct. It touched off a British civil war as supporters of William and James struggled for control of both Ireland and Scotland. By 1691 this had resulted in a Williamite triumph in both areas although neither could be regarded as completely pacified, and the Scottish Highlands remained tense as episodes such as the massacre of Glencoe of 1692 revealed.

A new order was created in each kingdom. The Episcopal order of the Church of Scotland was overturned in favour of a Presbyterian government. The Scots universities and schools were purged. As a result of procedural reforms in the 1690s the ability of the Edinburgh Parliament to take initiatives was enhanced and it took a number that revealed its independence of the executive. In Ireland the Catholic aspirations that had been encouraged during the reign of James II were crushed in the Protestant victory of the battle of the Boyne in 1690. English politicians did not doubt that Jacobite aspirations remained strong in both kingdoms. These were made more threatening by the possibility of French and Spanish assistance for the Jacobites.

French support had played a major role in the Irish resistance to Williamite conquest and in 1708 a French invasion force including James II's son, 'James III', nearly effected a landing on the east of Scotland.[1]

Scotland

Jacobitism and the strategic threat posed by Scotland and Ireland both engendered English concern and pushed together those politicians and groups in the three kingdoms who were opposed to Jacobitism. The Act of Union of 1707 arose essentially from English concern about the possible hazards posed by an autonomous, if not independent, Scotland. There was some support for the measure in Scotland, though its passage through the Scottish Parliament ultimately depended on corruption and self-interest. There was less need for a Union with Ireland. A shared anti-Catholicism helped keep the English government and the Parliament of Ireland in Dublin in rough harmony.

Union with England ensured that Scottish parliamentary politics would be waged in a Parliament (Westminster) where Scotland's representation was limited: 45 MPs and 16 representative peers out of 558 MPs and about 200 peers. As a result, Court and ministerial politics in London became more important for Scotland. Equally, it became necessary for English ministers seeking a secure parliamentary majority to control the votes of Scottish representatives and, therefore, the management of Scotland in a parliamentary sense became important. After 1707 Scotland was clearly a political as well as a security problem. This was exploited by Scottish politicians who sought to play the English party game in order to gain governmental patronage that would improve their position in London and Scotland.

Contemporary commentators were in no doubt of the importance of Scottish parliamentarians in Westminster. Vernon alleged in 1732 that the salt duty passed in the Commons 'merely by the weight of the Scots members'.[2] Henry Fox MP regarded their role as crucial in the fall of his patron Walpole: 'The Scotch are 24 against us and but 16 for us and there has been the Treachery.'

The comment of one Scottish MP, Gilbert Elliot, on an important division in 1755, 'Of the Scotch, few only were in the minority',[3] could have been repeated on many occasions. However, this role led to attention being given to their management and therefore to allegations of corruption. Lord Perceval wrote in 1715:

> I saw a warrant today signed by the king wherein were pensions granted to 19 Scotch Lords and 3 commoners, the highest was but £300 the lowest £100. Mr. Baron Scroop said that 6 of the 16 Scots peers chosen to sit in the present Parliament are included in another warrant, but their pensions are each £800. The rest have good employments. It may be truly said that nation is bought. £4000 used to buy their Parliament.[4]

The Scottish Presbyterian cleric Robert Wodrow complained in 1726 that the Scottish MPs had neglected Scotland's interests during the parliamentary debates over the malt tax:

> we now see under what influence our Members of Parliament are, and that they must be reimbursed in the charges they are at in their elections and attendance in Parliament; and it is much to be feared, the most part are influenced by pensions or hopes.[5]

The corruption of those elected, however injurious to Scottish confidence in their representatives, could not suffice for English politicians confronted by the willingness of their Scottish counterparts to align with English groups. This was utilised in order to secure the management of Scotland. In 1716 General Cadogan observed, 'the Scotch affairs have now so very near a connexion with the English ones'.[6] In 1708 the chief executive organ of government in Scotland, the Scottish Privy Council, had been abolished. Although the surviving Scottish officers of state sat in the British Privy Council, government policy was not formulated there, but rather in the Inner Cabinet, in which there was no Scottish member during the first half of the century. For much of the period, namely 1708–11, 1713–14, 1714–15, 1716–25 and 1742–6 there was a third Secretary of State responsible for Scotland. This post, held by major Scottish aristocrats, the last three being the Duke of Montrose (1714–15), the Duke of Roxburgh (1716–25) and the Marquis of Tweeddale (1742–6), did not confer control over all aspects of government in Scotland.

The officers of the revenue and of the armed forces were outside the Secretary's control, and the relevant ministers in London, therefore, wielded considerable power.

Walpole had no confidence in Roxburgh, who had backed Stanhope and Sunderland, and he blamed him for the disturbances in 1725 over the malt tax. The Scottish political crisis of 1725 led Walpole to seek an alliance with John, 2nd Duke of Argyll, and his brother Archibald Campbell, Earl of Ilay, and from 1743 until 1761 3rd Duke of Argyll. Though neither was made Scottish Secretary of State they managed Scotland for Walpole and, in turn, wielded most government patronage in Scotland. Ilay was responsible for most of the work of patronage. Charles Delafaye, an Under-Secretary of State, wrote of him in 1725, 'he seems singly to support His Majesty's authority and that of the laws'. A number of other aristocrats were, however, of some importance. The 3rd Earl of Loudoun was Commissioner to the General Assembly of the Church of Scotland and, as such, was instructed by George II in 1730 and 1731 'to suffer nothing to be done in the assembly to the prejudice of our authority or prerogative'.[7] Ilay remained loyal to Walpole after Argyll broke with him in 1740. Scottish management was thereafter disturbed for a number of years. The division in the Campbell family affected the general election results in 1741 and Carteret, when he gained office in 1742, supported the remains of the *Squadrone*, the Scottish Whig faction that had backed Stanhope and Sunderland, making the Marquis of Tweeddale Secretary of State for Scotland. However, the alliance between the Old Corps Whigs and the Campbells, created by Walpole, survived the challenge both of the *Squadrone* and of Jacobitism, and Ilay, now Duke of Argyll and the wealthiest Scottish peer, managed Scotland from 1746 until his death.[8]

In one important respect Scottish management was a failure. In 1745 most of Scotland easily fell to Bonnie Prince Charlie, Charles Edward the son of the Pretender, who raised the Highlands successfully, despite coming with only a tiny following. Stephen Poyntz, one-time governor of the Duke of Cumberland, reacted with concern to what he saw as a moral challenge:

That a nation like Scotland which makes the strictest profession of the Protestant Religion and values itself on respecting the sanctity of an oath should suffer the Pretender's son with a handful of rabble to walk the Protestant Succession out of that Kingdom, without lifting up a single weapon or hand against him, is astonishing to the last degree, and fills one with dreadful apprehensions for the behaviour of England, where a dissolute indifference for everything sacred and serious, and a luxurious impatience of dangers and hardships more generally prevails.[9]

A 'Memorial concerning the state of the Highlands and Islands of Scotland' published in a London Whig newspaper, the *Flying Post*, on 7 March 1723 had claimed that they were the greatest threat to Britain: 'as these people will never fail to join with foreign Popish powers, to advance the interests they have espoused; so they always have been, and infallibly will be instruments and tools in the hands of those who have a design to enslave or embroil the British nation.'

The article continued by casting a sceptical eye on government attempts to disarm the Highlands and by claiming that naval blockade would never be completely successful, both views that were to be vindicated in 1745. George I himself had in 1725 felt it necessary to recommend 'the careful execution of his orders by Major General Wade with respect to the disarming the Highlands'. Wade was instructed to continue the construction of fortifications and barracks in northern Scotland, Townshend writing: 'The King looks upon the securing that weak part as extremely necessary to discourage the Jacobites'.[10] Nevertheless, the failure of Jacobite risings and conspiracies between 1708 and 1722 and the settlement of the malt tax disturbances of 1725, which Walpole had followed closely, helped to diminish fears about Scotland.[11] Violence, such as the brawl at the public dinner held to celebrate the Roxburghshire election of 1726, when the newly elected MP killed a local gentleman who had not voted for him, was generally of a habitual kind, rather than aimed against the government. The Lord Advocate, Duncan Forbes, informed Newcastle in 1728 that disaffection 'was wearing out apace'.[12] In fact, Jacobitism was to revive from the late 1730s, in part because the monopolisation of patronage by the

Campbell interest left little practical recourse for loyal opposition. In 1726 Wodrow had queried: 'how far it be for the general interest of Scotland that we have a Scots secretary, since he must be of one of our sides, and so those of the other side [will] find much difficulty in their applications.' However, it is probable that there would have been no Jacobite rising but for British involvement in the War of the Austrian Succession. It was this which led Louis XV to plan an invasion in 1744 and to invite the Stuarts to France.[13] Bonnie Prince Charlie's march to Derby in 1745, the greatest crisis faced by the eighteenth-century British state, would have been even more serious had French forces invaded southern England as they planned to do and as the British ministry feared they would.

The suppression of the '45 was followed by a determined attempt to alter the political, social and strategic structure of the Highlands in order to make another rebellion impossible. The clans were disarmed and the clan system broken up, while roads to open up the Highlands and forts to awe them were constructed, a continuation of a policy that had led to regular expenditure during the Walpole years. Regalities and hereditable jurisdictions were abolished in pursuit of a policy explained in the title of an anonymous pamphlet, published in Edinburgh in 1746, *Superiorities displayed; or Scotland's grievance, by reason of the slavish dependence of the people upon their lands, and of the many hereditary jurisdictions over them. Wherein is shown, that these have been the handles of rebellion in preceding ages . . . and that, upon their removal, and putting the people of Scotland on the footing of those in England, the seeds of rebellion will be plucked up for ever.* The rebellion and its suppression gave cause and opportunity for the sort of radical state-directed action against some inherited privilege, especially regional and aristocratic privilege, that was so unusual in early eighteenth-century Europe and so rare in Britain.

Thereafter, the ministry in London devoted little attention to Scotland. Indeed, under Argyll's management, Scottish politics were less contentious in the 1750s than their London counterparts. Scotland made a major contribution to the British war effort in the Seven Years War. To the five specifically Scottish foot regiments in existence in 1756 at least another five were added. Charles Townshend, visiting Scotland at the end of the 1750s, was rhapsodical when he reported: 'it is a very rising country: industry is general: the improvements are rapid: the lowest rank of subjects is emancipated from traditional slavery: commerce driven from England by high taxes, luxury and abuse, seeks the simplicity, frugality and exemptions of Scotland, and this part of Britain must in time, from these causes succeed to the plenty, prosperity, cultivation, wealth, luxury, abuses and decline of England.'[14] Townshend was correct to note signs of economic development, while the Scottish poor law was regularly lauded also. Links between the two kingdoms, ranging from postal services to aristocratic intermarriage, improved.

The process was not always harmonious. Carteret had told the House of Lords in 1743 that: 'the people of this nation in particular have always been jealous of foreigners, nay, even of their fellow-subjects; for it is hardly possible to do justice to the Scottish or Irish, without raising a clamour among the English'.[15] The rise under George III of first Bute and later Lord Chief Justice Mansfield was accompanied by bitter denunciations of Scots who came south to make their fortune. 'They send us whole cargoes of their staple commodity, half-bred doctors and surgeons to poison and destroy our health' was one of the complaints of a correspondent of a London newspaper in 1771. However, these indications of tension were trivial compared to the fears of Scottish attack in 1745. Sir David Dalrymple observed in 1763: 'It has been often matter of astonishment to me why a minister in England should think a minister *here* necessary; we are so well broke, so thoroughly paced that we can be managed by a whipcord as well as by a double bridle, and yet the no-significancy of such tools serves in this country for talents and influence, and were that necessary, would supply the place of integrity likewise.' Scotland was no longer a security risk or particularly difficult to govern. If in 1761 a customs collector at Dumfries could report that gangs of smugglers numbering up to fifty were travelling inland with their goods in defiance of the outnumbered customs officers,[16] the position was no different along much of the eastern and southern coasts of England. Mentioning Scotland, the London newspaper *Common*

Sense reflected on 7 May 1737 that 'smaller dominions united to greater, no matter upon what terms . . . become dependent upon them'. This issue was essentially settled militarily in 1689, 1715, 1719 and 1745–6, not that the Jacobite cause simply opposed Scotland to England. Many Scots were firm opponents of the Stuarts and supporters of the Protestant Succession. To bolster this position, the half-century after the Union witnessed the development of a system of management in which patronage and shared interests replaced coercion. Force was replaced by necessary accommodation with leading Scots. The rewards for London included the need to keep few troops in Scotland and the overwhelming reliability of Scottish MPs. For Scotland the management of the 3rd Duke of Argyll brought a partisan patronage system but one directed by a Scot who was sensitive to Scottish interests and represented them in London. When Argyll died Scotland was not waiting to rebel and disaffection was limited.

Ireland

Whereas the number of Catholics in Scotland was small, they formed the majority of the population of Ireland. The seventeenth-century legacy of Catholic risings in Ireland and of Irish panics in England was such that sensitivity to events in Ireland, whether real or rumoured, was strong on the other side of the Irish Sea. There had been considerable concern when in 1689 the Dublin Parliament, composed almost wholly of Catholics and under the protection of James II, had rejected the right of Westminster to legislate for Ireland, vetoed appeals to England from Irish courts and repealed the Acts giving expression to the Restoration land settlements. The London press frequently referred to Catholic activity, proselytisation and acts of violence in Ireland, the *General Evening Post* of 12 February 1734, for example, reporting that in Meath, 'information of many Polish priests, friars and monasteries, not heard of till this enquiry', had been discovered. The recruiting of Irishmen for the Irish regiments in French service caused particular concern in the

1730s, and was a tricky issue in 1730 when the two powers were allies. Newcastle confided to his brother his conviction that 'we shall have it in Parliament, and when it comes there, I believe it will be more universally blamed, even by our own friends, than anything we have done'.[17]

The Jacobites were optimistic about their support in Ireland and in 1731 the French *chargé d'affaires* in London reported that Ireland, treated tyrannically as it was, was in despair.[18] However, Delafaye was to be proved correct in his view, expressed in 1725: 'I can have no notion of a scheme of our enemies upon Ireland where there is an army, and where all the Protestants (in whose hands is the wealth and power), bad as they are, are so nearly concerned in point of private interest to resist such an attempt.'[19] The Protestant Ascendancy was strongly established. Under the Banishment Act of 1697 hundreds of Catholic clerics had been banished under pain of execution if they returned. The castration of Catholic clerics was subsequently considered. Under the penal statutes passed in the first half of the eighteenth century Catholics were prevented from freely acquiring or bequeathing land or property and were disfranchised and debarred from all political, military and legal offices. In 1691 Catholics were disqualified from sitting in the Dublin Parliament; in 1727 from voting in elections to it. Acts forbade mixed marriages, Catholic schools and the bearing of arms by Catholics. It has been estimated that the percentage of land in Catholic hands fell from 59 in 1641 to 22 in 1688, 14 in 1703 and 5 in 1778, though some of the Protestant ownership was only token.

The Penal Code was designed essentially to destroy the political and economic power of Catholicism rather than the faith itself. The ability of the Anglican establishment to proselytise was limited by its general failure to communicate with a still largely Gaelic-speaking population. In contrast, the Catholic colleges stipulated a knowledge of that language as a requirement for the mission. The Catholic percentage of the population did not diminish, because the Catholic clergy, wearing secular dress and secretly celebrating mass, continued their work, sustained by a strong oral culture, the emotional link with a sense of national identity, by hedge-school teaching and by a fair amount of tacit government acceptance. Serious repression was episodic. If it had been possible to implement the religious clauses of the Penal Code and if a persistent attempt had been made to do so, then Catholicism might have been seriously challenged, though the military forces in the island were not large and the result in 1715 and 1745 might have been Jacobite insurrections. Instead, a crucial feature of both years was that there was no Irish rising despite the continued tradition of Jacobitism among the majority of the population. 'The numbers of Roman Catholics in Ireland' was one reason why James Craggs, one of the Secretaries of State, feared that a Spanish pro-Jacobite invasion force would be directed there in 1719.[20] Catholic clerics in Ireland still prayed for 'James III' in the 1730s, as did Scottish Episcopalians, and the draconian Irish wartime legislation of 1697, 1703–4 and 1709 was inspired by fears of Catholic disloyalty and links with France, though persecution usually slackened in peacetime. However, long-standing religious grievances helped to exacerbate political disaffection in the 1790s.

Though the Protestant Ascendancy in Ireland, centred on the Parliament in Dublin, had a shared interest with England in keeping Ireland quiet, this did not prevent problems from developing in the relationship between London and Dublin. Viewed from Westminster, management was not free of difficulties, even though London was firmly in control. The executive in Dublin Castle, headed by the Lord Lieutenant, was appointed from London and responsible to British officers of state. The crown enjoyed a large 'hereditary revenue' in Ireland. The Irish Parliament had no right to prepare legislation, that being the task of the Irish Privy Council, whose bills had to be approved by the Privy Council in London. The Westminster Parliament itself also possessed the power to legislate for Ireland. Its Declaratory Act of 1720 declared its 'full power and authority to make Laws and Statutes . . . to bind the Kingdom and People of Ireland', and denied to the Irish House of Lords any appellate jurisdiction from the Irish courts.[21]

England's constitutional and political dominance led to measures that aroused anger in Ireland. The granting of Irish lands and pensions to favoured courtiers in London exacerbated the problem of absentee landowners and revenue-holders with the consequent drain of money out of the country.[22] Legislation in Westminster, the result of persistent protectionist lobbying by the English woollen interest, hindered Irish wool exports, one pamphlet complaining in 1731 'it is as well to be hanged as starved'.[23] In 1722 a Wolverhampton ironmaster, William Wood, purchased a patent to mint copper coins for Ireland, a measure that aroused a storm of complaint in Ireland where it was seen as a threat to the economy and a consequence of Ireland's vulnerable constitutional position. The controversy created serious difficulties for the officials and politicians in Dublin. In 1724 Townshend noted that he had received from William Conolly, Speaker of the Irish House of Commons 1715–29, his:

> answer to the orders that have been lately sent him in relation to the new coinage. He says that as Commissioner of the Revenue he is bound to follow any directions he receives from His Majesty, but as his acting immediately in consequence of those orders, may lay him under some difficulties as Speaker of the House of Commons, he desires a little time to consider of some expedient to reconcile those two characters.[24]

In 1722, a London newspaper, the *British Journal*, in its issue of 24 November, had called for a reform in the way that Ireland was governed 'when our superiors are at leisure from greater affairs'. Pressing the need to preserve the dependence of the colonies, the paper argued that Ireland was:

> too powerful to be treated only as a colony; and that if we design to continue them friends, the best way to do it, is to imitate the example of merchants and shopkeepers; that is, when their apprentices are acquainted with their trade and their customers, and are out of their time, to take them into partnership, rather than to set them up for themselves in their neighbourhood.

There was to be no partnership, at least for the bulk of the Irish population, but the relationship between London and Ireland was not as one-sided as the constitutional arrangements might suggest. The Irish Parliament had to be managed, not least because of the need to finance the military budget, and Lord Lieutenants such as the Duke of Bolton in 1717[25] were very concerned about the difficulties that this posed. The solution was to use Irish political managers who were known as 'undertakers' and this introduced a further element of compromise. Furthermore, Irish politicians could seek to influence policy in London by lobbying[26] and by their links with British politicians. The latter played a role in the divisions in Irish politics in the reign of Anne and George I, with a Whig–Tory divide being followed by a Whig triumph in the general election of 1715 and a subsequent Whig split in which a struggle for office was central.

This division persisted into the early 1720s, Lord Chancellor Midleton looking to Carteret for support against the Duke of Grafton, Lord Lieutenant 1720–4, and Walpole. In combination with the storm over Wood's Halfpence, this produced a difficult situation that was solved by the replacement of Grafton by Carteret, a move that Walpole hoped would wreck him,[27] the fall of Midleton and the recall of Wood's patent. Although intended primarily to ease Walpole's position at Court, by removing Carteret from a position, a Secretaryship of State, in which he could develop royal favour, the changes of 1724–5 helped to quieten Irish politics. Divisions and disputes did not cease but there was to be no political crisis compelling the attention of London comparable to that of 1722–5 for the rest of the Walpole ministry, though Walpole continued to keep an eye on Irish politics.[28] Carteret's successors, the Duke of Dorset (1730–7) and the Duke of Devonshire (1737–45), lacked his ability and political skills, but an essential harmony of interest combined with the deployment of government patronage by Irish undertakers helped to keep Ireland and the Anglo-Irish relationship fundamentally stable. An official in Dublin was able to write in 1742 to a counterpart in London: 'Our Parliament have acted with great unanimity and gave the supply with great cheerfulness. I am glad I can tell you that his Grace has had as easy a session of Parliament as ever was known, I wish your Parliament when they meet would act after the same manner'. The situation was just as peaceful in 1744.[29]

This stability was to dissolve slowly after the '45 with the growth of Protestant Irish patriotism and constitutional sensitivity. In 1753–6 the 'Money Bill Dispute', a quarrel over whether the Crown or the Dublin Parliament had the right to dispose of a surplus in the Irish Treasury arising from Irish taxation, led to a bitter and wide-ranging controversy. The removal of the external and internal threat of Jacobitism led to a change in the Anglo-Irish relationship and a reassessment of attitudes that was to provide the context for a series of political and constitutional disputes. In a similar fashion the crushing of the French threat to Britain's North American colonies during the Seven Years War helped to prepare the ground for post-war constitutional disputes between these colonies and London. No constitution was so watertight as to preclude the possibility of disputes, and the ambiguous processes of compromise that constituted such a large part of government and patronage were subject in periods of tension to comparable difficulties.

The stability of the British Isles

One of the major problems confronting the rulers and governments of many European states was their relationship with regions where their authority and power were especially circumscribed. The nature of the problem varied greatly and was understandably less serious for minor states. In all large states, however, the problem existed, particularly with respect to regions gained through conquest and dynastic succession in which local privileges and a sense of separate identity had been preserved. This was not invariably the case. The Swedish region of Ingria was conquered by Peter the Great of Russia during the Great Northern War (1700–21), later becoming the province of St Petersburg. During the war most of the landowners left or were expelled and Peter, acknowledging no prior right of ownership, began settlement and development policies accordingly. Such policies were, however, common only in eastern Europe, in cases of colonial expansion, and in the wake of rebellions which had been suppressed without negotiation.

Local privileges and a sense of separate identity were of scant value to the Irish Catholics, or to the Scottish Highlanders after the '45. The substantial emigration of Irish Catholic gentry under the terms of the Treaty of Limerick (1691) reflected their recognition that they had little future in Ireland, as did the subsequent emigration of Irish Catholics to seek their fortune abroad, not least by service in foreign armies. About 11,000 Irish left the country soon after the treaty. By 1749 only 8 out of 114 Irish peers were Catholics. However, for the politically involved groups, at least, a sense of separate identity and national privileges played a significant role in the relationship between on the one hand England and on the other Scotland and Ireland, though not Wales. Ireland retained its Parliament, Scotland had a different national church and legal system and both Ireland and Scotland required specialised management. Hostility to Jacobitism linked the Irish and Scottish political establishments, as remodelled after 1714, to London, producing a pressure for co-operation distinct from the customary aspirations that eased the path of management. In addition, the sense of separate identity was attenuated, especially at the level of the social and political elite, by the decline of the Celtic languages and the growing appeal of English cultural norms and customs. Welsh, Irish and Scots sought to benefit from links with England, a process facilitated by the spread of English. The decline of a separate cultural identity, for example among the Welsh gentry of Glamorgan after about 1740, played an important, though intangible role, in the increasing hegemony of English ideas. Although the Irish Protestant elite became more conscious of a possible national role, they continued to identify culturally with England rather than with the bulk of the Irish population. The Welsh and Scottish landed elite became increasingly Anglo-centric. This played a major role in the growing British stability which was such a notable feature of the century until the 1770s, when developments in Ireland made the relationship between England and Ireland more contentious and difficult. Had the '45 succeeded, then it would have been foolish to write of growing stability, but the increased acceptance and exploitation of England's cultural hegemony helped to ensure that there were no more '45s.

CONCLUSION

Commenting on Walpole's position in the Commons, Sarah Marlborough snapped: 'I really think that they might pass an act there, if they pleased, to take away Magna Carta'.[1] On the other hand, 'Medium', a character in a London play of 1737, reflected: 'He out of office shall often oppose to be employed; and the man in post shall be restive to rise higher! – Well! of all men living, I think a primier [sic] Minister the most wretched'.[2]

Though both Walpole's ministerial position and longevity and the Whig ascendancy in general were ascribed by many contemporary critics to corruption, both on the part of those who offered bribes and of those who took them, it is clear that political management involved far more than that. The policies that were followed and the abilities of those who wielded power must be considered. Partly because Walpole's abilities were primarily financial and parliamentary, it was natural to suspect and emphasise the role of money in bolstering his position. Robert Wodrow was in no doubt in 1724 that Walpole's financial acumen and political standing were interrelated:

> Mr Walpole at present manages all . . . he has raised his reputation and interest exceedingly by his dealings with the Dutch. The moneyed people there have a high value for him, because of his appearances in the end of the Queen's [Anne] reign in favour of liberty, and are willing to trust their money in his hands at three per cent. This put him in case to deal with the three great companys in England, the Bank, India, and the South Sea, and

to bring them to his own terms, as to the national debt, and being thus in case to guide these three, and consequently the House of Commons, he is got to the head of affairs, and is become absolutely necessary to the King, and is like to continue so till some new turn happen.[3]

Seven years later Chavigny was blunter:

Mr Walpole is absolute. He wields the royal authority and controls the money and has the one by the other. Never has any English minister lasted for so long but, because of that, he has more to fear. His adherents are not all his supporters and his friends.[4]

It was easy for critics, both contemporary and later, to underrate the value of stability, to forget the fragility of government, the precariousness of civil peace and the danger of international failure. Ministerial spokesmen stressed the inevitable fallibility of all government. Lord Chancellor Hardwicke told the Lords in December 1740 that 'every human establishment has its advantages and its inconveniences'. He also argued that political disputes were an integral part of a free government and not, therefore, a proof of crisis, telling the Lords in February 1741, 'in every country where a free government is established, every time must be a time of political altercation'.[5]

This argument is worthy of attention. A political system without dispute was hardly to be expected. Indeed, the problems facing the government, ranging from the Jacobite challenge and the difficult international situation to the primitive economy which kept much of the population in a precarious state exposed, as in 1740, to the consequences of poor harvests, were such that any assumption about an inevitable growth in stability must appear facile. Walpole was well aware of the many and varied dangers posed by instability and conflict. By stressing the fragility and precariousness of the Hanoverian position, recent historical work is only now opening up a perspective in which more emphasis has to be placed on the political skills of those who maintained domestic peace, and more value can be attached to the simple task of keeping the show going, of providing a peaceful structure for political activity and government action.

Naturally, peace and stability were not simply due to political leadership. Social and economic developments were also important although the first half of the century was not a period of marked growth and it was arguably the political achievement of peace and, therefore, lower taxes that helped to increase the disposable wealth of the community rather than growth. The political achievement of the Walpole ministry should not be underrated. It can be measured in large part by the difficulties of the period 1714–20 and 1742–8. There was nothing inevitable in the transition that occurred from conspiracy and battlefield to elections and parliamentary government, so that in 1762 the blue-stocking Elizabeth Montagu could reflect: 'a virtuoso or a dilletanti may stand as secure in these times behind his Chinese rail as the knight on his battlements in former days'.[6] This political achievement owed much in England to Walpole while in Britain as a whole it was based both on shared interests among landowners and on the threat and use of force against Jacobites.

REFERENCES

Abbreviations

Add.	Additional Manuscripts
AE.CP.Ang.	Paris, Ministère des Affaires Etrangères, Correspondence Politique Angleterre
Beinecke	New Haven, Yale University, Beinecke Library
BL	London, British Library
Bodl.	Oxford, Bodleian Library
Cobbett	W. Cobbett, *Parliamentary History of England* (36 vols., 1806–20)
CRO	County Record Office
CUL	Cambridge, University Library
HL	San Marino, California, Huntington Library
HMC	Historical Manuscripts Commission
Harrowby	Sandon Hall, archive of Earl Harrowby, papers of Dudley Ryder
LO	Loudoun papers
NLS	Edinburgh, National Library of Scotland
(ns)	New Style
PRO	London, Public Record Office, State Papers
RA	Windsor, Royal Archives, Stuart Papers
SRO	Edinburgh, Scottish Record Office
Walpole corresp.	Correspondence of Horace Walpole and Horace Mann. Edited by W. S. Lewis in *The Yale Edition of Horace Walpole's Correspondence* (New Haven, 1937–83)

Unless otherwise noted, the place of publication for all books is London.

PREFACE

1. BL Egerton Mss 1711 f.184.

1 WALPOLE'S RISE

1. BL Add. 64928 f.53.
2. Speech at Sacheverell's trial, BL Add. 9131 f.8–9.
3. H. Davis (ed.), *The Prose Writings of Jonathan Swift* (14 vols, Oxford, 1939–68), X, 84.
4. *The Reader*, 3 May 1714; Anon., *A Letter to the Right Honourable Robert Walpole* (1716), p. 6; Anon., The *Woeful Treaty* (London, 1716), p. 4; Anon., *The Character and Principles of the Present Set of Whigs* (London, 1711), p. 15.
5. Robert Arbuthnot to Earl of Stair, 30 May 1717, SRO GD 135/141/11; B. Williams, *Stanhope* (Oxford, 1932), pp. 230–52; J. H. Plumb, *Sir Robert Walpole: The Making of a Statesman* (1956), pp. 222–42; J. M. Beattie, *The English Court in the Reign of George I* (Cambridge, 1967), pp. 225–40; J. J. Murray, *George I, the Baltic and the Whig Split of 1717* (1969); W. A. Speck, 'The Whig Schism under George I', *Huntington Library Quarterly*, XL (1977), 171–9; R. Hatton, *George I* (London, 1978), pp. 193–202; C. Jones, 'The Impeachment of the Earl of Oxford and the Whig Schism', *Bulletin of the Institute of Historical Research*, LV (1982), 66–87; R. Hatton, 'New Light on George I', in S. Baxter (ed.), *England's Rise to Greatness 1660–1763* (Berkeley, 1983), pp. 230–2; J. M. Black; 'Parliament and the Political and Diplomatic Crisis of 1717–1718', *Parliamentary History*, III (1984), 77–102.
6. R. Hatton, *George I*, p. 246.
7. *Daily Courant*, 19 Jan. 1734.
8. Anon., *The Doctrine of Innuendo's Discussed* (1731), pp. 16–17; *Craftsman*, 10 Feb. 1727.
9. BL Add. 37367 f.303.
10. BL Add. 47028 f.257; G. M. Townend, 'Religious Radicalism and Conservatism in the Whig Party under George I: The Repeal of the Occasional Conformity and Schism Acts', *Parliamentary History*, VII (1988), 24–44.
11. SRO GD 220/5268; William Bell to Thomas Clutterbuck, 10 Jan. 1719, Gloucester CRO D149 F18; *An Epistle to R– W–* (1718), p. 21.
12. J. F. Naylor (ed.), *The British Aristocracy and the Peerage Bill of 1719*

(New York, 1968); J. M. Black, 'Regulating Oxford: Ministerial Intentions in 1719', *Oxoniensia*, L (1985), 283–5.

13. PRO 43/4 f.119–20, 150, 227.

14. BL Add. 47028 f.133; Surrey CRO 1248/3 f.307.

15. E. Cruickshanks, *Political Untouchables: The Tories and the '45* (1979); L. J. Colley, *In Defiance of Oligarchy: The Tory Party, 1714–1760* (Cambridge, 1982); I. R. Christie, 'The Tory Party, Jacobitism and the "Forty-Five",' *Historical Journal*, 30 (1987), 921–31; Cruickshanks, 'Religion and Royal Succession – The Rage of Party', in C. Jones (ed.), *Britain in the First Age of Party 1680–1750* (1987), pp. 19–43; Cruickshanks and Black (eds), *The Jacobite Challenge* (Edinburgh, 1988); P. Monod, '"For the King to Enjoy His Own Again". Jacobite Political Culture in England, 1688–1788' (Yale, PhD, 1985).

16. P. Fritz, 'The Anti-Jacobite Intelligence System of the English Ministers, 1715–1745', *Historical Journal*, 16 (1973), 265–89; Fritz, *The English Ministers and Jacobitism between the Rebellions of 1715 and 1745* (Toronto, 1975); Black, 'British Intelligence and the Mid-Eighteenth Century Crisis', *Intelligence and National Security*, 2 (1987), 209–29.

17. BL Add. 32686 f.153.

18. PRO 43/4 f.116; BL Add. 32686 f.285.

19. HL LO 8344; J. Black, 'An "Ignoramus" in European affairs?', *British Journal for Eighteenth-Century Studies*, 6 (1983), 55–65; Black, *British Foreign Policy in the Age of Walpole* (Edinburgh, 1985).

20. G. V. Bennett, *The Tory Crisis in Church and State, 1688–1730: The Career of Francis Atterbury Bishop of Rochester* (Oxford, 1975); R. Davis, 'The "Presbyterian" opposition and the emergence of party in the House of Lords in the reign of Charles II' in C. Jones (ed.), *Party and Management in Parliament, 1660–1784* (Leicester, 1984), pp. 1–35; J. C. D. Clark, *English Society 1688–1832* (Cambridge, 1985).

21. BL Add. 62558 f.80.

22. T. F. J. Kendrick, 'Sir Robert Walpole, the Old Whigs and the Bishops, 1733–1736: A Study in Eighteenth Century Parliamentary Politics', *Historical Journal*, 11 (1968), 421–45; S. Taylor, 'Sir Robert Walpole, the Church of England, and the Quakers Tithe Bill of 1736', *Historical Journal*, 28 (1985), 51–77.

23. BL Add. 47029 f.132; RA 103/80.

24. G. F. Nuttall (ed.), *Calendar of the Correspondence of Philip Doddridge* (1979), p. 355.

25. Wellcome Institute, London. Mss 5006, p. 34; Walpole corresp. 4,167.

26. Newcastle to Carteret, 3 June 1743, PRO 43/34.

27. RA 103/80.

28. E. R. Turner, 'The Excise Scheme of 1733', *English Historical Review*, 42 (1927), 54–7; P. Langford, *The Excise Crisis* (Oxford, 1975); M. Jubb, 'Economic Policy and Economic Development', in J. Black (ed.), *Britain in the Age of Walpole* (1984), pp. 121–44; J. M. Price, 'The Excise Affair Revisited: The Administrative and Colonial Dimensions of a Parliamentary Crisis' in S. Baxter (ed.), *England's Rise to Greatness* (Berkeley, 1983), pp. 257–321.

29. D. Baugh, *British Naval Administration in the Age of Walpole* (Princeton, 1965); P. G. M. Dickson, *The Financial Revolution in England* (1967).

30. W. R. Ward, *The English Land Tax in the Eighteenth Century* (Oxford, 1953).

31. N. Landau, *The Justices of the Peace 1679–1760* (Berkeley, 1984); S. Baskerville, 'The Management of the Tory Interest in Lancashire and Cheshire, 1714–47' (Oxford, DPhil, 1976), appendix.

32. R. R. Sedgwick (ed.), *The History of Parliament. The House of Commons 1715–54* (2 vols, 1970), I, 33–50; B. W. Hill, *The Growth of Parliamentary Parties 1689–1742* (1976), pp. 189–226.

33. BL Add. 47028 f.7.

34. J. P. Kenyon, *Revolution Principles: The Politics of Party 1689–1720* (Cambridge, 1977).

2 STABILITY, PATRONAGE AND PARLIAMENT

1. HL LO 7634; J. H. Plumb, *The Growth of Political Stability in England, 1675–1725* (1967); G. Holmes, 'The Achievement of Stability: the Social Context of Politics from the 1680s to the Age of Walpole', in J. Cannon (ed.), *The Whig Ascendancy* (1981), pp. 1–22, reprinted in Holmes, *Politics, Religion and Society in England, 1679–1742* (1986), pp. 249–79; Holmes, *Augustan England: Professions, State and Society 1680–1730* (1982).

2. J. R. Kenyon, *Revolution Principles*, p. 204; L. J. Colley, *Defiance of Oligarchy*, p. 21.

3. Cruickshanks, 'Religion and Royal Succession – The Rage of Party', in Jones (ed.), *Britain in the First Age of Party* (1987), p. 41.

4. D. Hay, P. Linebaugh and E. P. Thompson, *Albion's Fatal Tree. Crime and Society in Eighteenth-Century England* (1975); Thompson, *Whigs and Hunters: The Origin of the Black Act* (1975); N. Rogers, 'The Urban Opposition to Whig Oligarchy, 1720–60', in M. and

J. Jacob (eds), *The Origins of Anglo-American Radicalism* (1984), pp. 132–48.

5. PRO 43/4 f.244.
6. Thompson, 'The Moral Economy of the English Crowd in the Eighteenth Century', *Past and Present*, 50 (1971); J. Stevenson, *Popular Disturbances in England 1700–1870* (1979); J. Brewer and J. Styles (eds), *An Ungovernable People: The English and their Law in the Seventeenth and Eighteenth Centuries* (1980); Rogers, 'Riot and Popular Jacobitism in Early Hanoverian England' in Cruickshanks (ed.), *Ideology and Conspiracy: Aspects of Jacobitism, 1689–1759* (Edinburgh, 1982), pp. 70–88; Kenyon, *Revolution Principles*, p. 204.
7. Dickson, *Financial Revolution*, pp. 9–10, 80, 82, 209–10; Anon., *Outlines of a Plan of Finance* (London, 1813), p. 1.
8. SRO GD 150/3474/56; Cobbett, X, 74–187; Dickson, *Financial Revolution*, pp. 212–15.
9. S. Varey (ed.), *Lord Bolingbroke. Contributions to the 'Craftsman'* (Oxford, 1982); J. Andrew, *A Comparative View of the French and English Nations* (1785), pp. 47–8.
10. *Universal Daily Register*, 10 Aug. 1786; Thicknesse, *Useful Hints to those who make the Tour of France* (1768), p. 130.
11. *Monitor*, 5 Aug. 1758, 9 July 1763; *The Contrast*, 10 Aug. 1763.
12. *Walpole corresp.* Walpole to Mann 26 Aug. 1785; BL Add. 23810 f.481; Lowther to John Spedding, 18 May 1742, Carlisle, Cumbria RO D/Lons/W.
13. NLS MS. 14221 f.186–7.
14. Harrowby, Ryder diary, 13 Feb. 1741; Anon., *Letters from the Westminster Journal* (1747), iii–iv.
15. Sparre to Count Horn, the Swedish first minister, 15 June 1733, PRO 107/13.
16. SRO GD 18/5245/4/14.
17. BL Add. 51345 f.3; Bedford Record Office L 30/8/39/20; E. J. Climenson (ed.), *Passages from the Diaries of Mrs Philip Lybbe Powys* (1899), p. 6; Harrowby, Ryder diary, 18 Oct. 1739.
18. Harley, parliamentary diary, CUL Add. 6851 f.89–90.
19. BL Add. 37388 f.301.
20. BL Add. 32686 f.193.
21. PRO 43/4 f.150, 292; Bodl. MS A. 269, pp. 99–100. C. Realey, *The Early Opposition to Sir Robert Walpole* (Philadelphia, 1931).
22. PRO 43/5 f.111.
23. H. T. Dickinson, *Bolingbroke* (London, 1970).
24. RA 97/110.
25. HMC, *Onslow*, pp. 516–17; Peter, Lord King, 'Notes on Domestic

and Foreign Affairs during the last years of the reign of George I and the early part of the reign of George II', in appendix to P. King, *Life of John Locke* (2 vols, 1830), II, p. 46.

26. Cardinal Fleury, French first minister, to George II, 2 July (ns) 1727, PRO 100/17.

27. Le Coq to Augustus II of Saxony, 22 July (ns) 1727, Dresden, Haupstaatsarchiv, Geheimes Kabinett, Gesandtschaften 2676, vol. 18 a.

28. Black, 'Fresh Light on the Fall of Townshend', *Historical Journal*, 29 (1986), pp. 41–64; Black, 'Additional Light on the Fall of Townshend', *Yale University Library Gazette* (1989).

29. G. H. Rose (ed.), *A Selection from the Papers of the Earls of Marchmont* (3 vols, 1831), II, p. 233; Beinecke, Osborn Shelves, Stair Letters No. 51.

30. *Wyes Letter*, 21 Aug. 1733; Maidstone, Kent Archive Office U269 C 148/12, 23.

31. Wasner to Sinzendorf, 5 Oct. (ns) 1734, Vienna, Haus, Hof und Staatsarchiv, Englische Korrespondenz 70; Ossorio to Charles Emmanuel III, 16 Jan. (ns) 1735, Turin, Archivio di Stato, Lettere Ministri Inghilterra 42.

32. BL Add. 47033 f.62; C. S. Cowper (ed.), *The Diary of Mary, Countess Cowper 1714–1720* (1864), p. 164; Black, *The Collapse of the Anglo-French Alliance 1727–1731* (Gloucester, 1987), pp. 19–20.

33. Walpole to the Duke of Devonshire, 4 Dec. 1737, Chatsworth, Devonshire Mss, 1st series Box 2, 114.9.

34. P. Woodfine, 'The Anglo-Spanish War of 1739', in Black (ed.), *The Origins of War in Early-Modern Europe* (Edinburgh, 1987), pp. 185–209.

35. I. G. Doolittle, 'A first-hand account of the Commons debate on the removal of Sir Robert Walpole, 13 February 1741', *Bulletin of the Institute of Historical Research*, 53 (1980), 125–40.

36. BL Add. 32693 f.472; SRO GD 248.48/1.

37. BL Add. 23810 f.101; Morton to Duncan Forbes, 23 Jan. 1742, *More Culloden papers*, 3 (Inverness, 1927).

38. Harrowby, Ryder diary, 16 Feb. 1740.

39. HMC, *Diary of the First Earl of Egmont* (3 vols, 1920–3), II, 150; *St. James's Chronicle*, 18 Ap. 1769; Marburg, Staatsarchiv, 4 f. England 344, report of 30 Jan. 1770.

40. Taunton, Somerset RO, Dd/SAS f.A41 C/795, letter from George Harbin 19 Dec. 1741.

41. HMC, *Egmont*, III, 239.

42. J. B. Owen, *The Rise of the Pelhams* (London, 1957), pp. 1–40.

43. Bodl. MS Eng. Lett. c144 f.58.

44. Beinecke, Osborn Shelves, Stair Letters No. 54.
45. Cobbett, XIII, 567.
46. CUL Add. 6851 vol. 2 f.47.
47. NLS 7046 f.38.
48. SRO GD 150/3485/46; Walpole corresp. III, 34.
49. Chichester, West Sussex CRO Goodwood Mss 104 No. 276, T. J. McCann, *The Correspondence of the Dukes of Richmond and Newcastle 1724–1750* (Lewes, 1984), p. 124.
50. Harrowby, 21 R.144.
51. W. Coxe, *Memoirs of the Life and Administration of Sir Robert Walpole, Earl of Orford* (3 vols, 1798), III, 592.
52. PRO 30/29/1/11 f.285; Earl Gower to Pelham, 15 Oct. 1743, Nottingham University Library, NeC 113.
53. Cobbett, XIII, 467n; CUL Add. 6851 vol. 2 f.70.
54. Coxe, *Memoirs of the Administration of the Right Honourable Henry Pelham* (2 vols, 1829); J. W. Wilkes, *A Whig in Power: The Political Career of Henry Pelham* (Northwestern University Press, 1964); A. Newman, 'Henry Pelham', in H. van Thal (ed.), *The Prime Ministers* (2 vols, 1974), I, pp. 61–71.
55. BL Egerton Mss 1711 f.184.
56. AE. Mémoires et Documents Angleterre 6 f.101; Coxe, *Memoirs . . . Orford*, III, 168.
57. BL Add. 32686 f.300, 312–13; PRO 43/4 f.203, 211; Plumb, *Sir Robert Walpole: The King's Minister* (1960), pp. 91–102.
58. BL Althorp Mss B3, 14 Ap. 1726.
59. Lonsdale to Fleming, 30 Oct. 1737, Carlisle, Cumbria RO, D/Sen./Fleming 14; SRO GD 248/48/1; HL LO 7902; BL Add. 63470 f.154.
60. PRO 41/15 f/ 272.
61. *Old England*, 9 Feb. 1745.
62. Cobbett, XI, 224.
63. W. Mure (ed.), *Selections from the Family Papers preserved at Caldwell* (Glasgow, 1854), p. 233; Surrey CRO, Brodrick Mss, 1248/4 f.222, 377; New Haven, Yale University, Beinecke Library, Osborn Shelves c201 No. 1.
64. P. Stanhope, 4th Earl of Chesterfield, *Characters* (1778), p. 31.
65. P. Yorke, 2nd Earl of Hardwicke, *Walpoliana* (1781), p. 17.
66. R. Sedgwick (ed.), John, Lord Hervey, *Some Materials towards Memoirs of the Reign of George II* (3 vols, 1931), I, pp. 177–8.
67. SRO GD 150/3476/101.
68. BL Add. 62558 f.4–5.
69. Anon., *A Defence of the People* (1744), p. 80.
70. BL Add. 47033 f.59; RA 103/80.

71. Frederick William I to Andrié, 24 May 1739, PRO 107/24.
72. Harrowby, vol. 432 Doc 30 B.
73. Walpole to Sir Thomas Lowther, 2 Jan. 1731, Walpole to Sir John Ramsden, 5 Nov. 1741, Carlisle, DD Ca 22/1/3, D/Pen/234.
74. Walpole to Townshend, 26 June 1723, PRO 43/66; PRO 43/4 f.98; Walpole to Lord Malton, 6 Nov. 1739, Sheffield Public Library, Wentworth Woodhouse Mss M3; C. Jones, 'The House of Lords and the Growth of Parliamentary Stability, 1701–1742' in Jones (ed.), *Britain in the First Age of Party* (1987), pp. 100–1; Black, 'The House of Lords and British Foreign Policy, 1720–48' in C. Jones (ed.), *A Pillar of the Constitution. The House of Lords in British Politics, 1640–1784* (1989), pp. 113–36.
75. Surrey CRO Brodrick Mss 1248/7 f.19.
76. J. C. Collins, *Voltaire, Montesquieu and Rousseau in England* (1908); G. Bonno, 'La Culture and la civilisation britanniques devant l'opinion française de la Paix d'Utrecht aux "Lettres Philosophiques" 1713–34', *Transactions of the American Philosophical Society* (1948); R. Shackleton, *Montesquieu* (Oxford, 1961).
77. BL Add. 37388 f.193; 35363 f.26–7.
78. *Whitehall Journal*, 4 Dec. 1722; Anon. *Liberty and the Craftsman* (1730), p. 5; *Daily Courant*, 5 Oct. 1734.
79. *London Journal*, 1 Aug. 1724; *Weekly Register*, 4 Sept. 1731.
80. *London Journal*, 9 Feb. 1723.
81. D. W. Jones, *War and Economy in the Age of William III and Marlborough* (Oxford, 1988).

3 THE CROWN AND THE POLITICAL NATION

1. Black, *British Foreign Policy in the Age of Walpole* (Edinburgh, 1985), pp. 27–48.
2. J. B. Owen, 'George II Reconsidered', in J. S. Bromley, P. G. M. Dickson and A. Whiteman (eds), *Statesmen, Scholars and Merchants* (Oxford, 1973), pp. 113–34.
3. HL STG Box 191 (12).
4. R. Hatton, *George I* (1978); E. Gregg, *Queen Anne* (London, 1980); J. C. D. Clark, *The Dynamics of Change: The Crisis of the 1750s and English Party Systems* (Cambridge, 1982); P. Mackesy, *War without Victory* (Oxford, 1984).
5. Churchill College Cambridge, Erle-Drax Mss 2/12.
6. C. Roberts, 'Party and Patronage in Later Stuart England', in Baxter (ed.), *England's Rise to Greatness*, p. 205.

7. AE.CP.Ang. 259 f.39; BL Add. 32686 f.175.
8. SRO GD 150/3474/21.
9. Black, 'Parliament and Foreign Policy in the Age of Walpole: the case of the Hessians', in Black (ed.), *Knights Errant and True Englishmen: British Foreign Policy, 1660–1800* (Edinburgh, 1989), pp. 41–54.
10. Horatio Walpole to Walpole, 10 Oct. 1738, Sheffield Public Library, Wentworth Woodhouse Mss M3.
11. M. Peters, 'Pitt as a foil to Bute: the public debate over ministerial responsibility and the powers of the Crown', in K. Schweizer (ed.), *Lord Bute. Essays in Re-interpretation* (Leicester, 1988), p. 111.
12. Owen, *The Rise of the Pelhams* (1957), pp. 159–297.
13. R. Sedgwick (ed.), John, Lord Hervey, *Some Materials towards Memoirs of the Reign of George II* (3 vols, 1931), particularly pp. 261, 750–2.
14. Owen, 'George II Reconsidered'; Black, 'George II Reconsidered', *Mitteilungen des Österreichischen Staatsarchiv*, 35 (1982), pp. 35–56.
15. G. Holmes, *British Politics in the Age of Anne* (1967), pp. 440–2; B. W. Hill, *Robert Harley* (1988), p. 239.
16. M. Thomson, *The Secretaries of State, 1681–1782* (Oxford, 1932).
17. M. Harris, 'Print and Politics in the Age of Walpole', in Black (ed.), *Britain in the Age of Walpole* (1984), pp. 189–210; Black, *The English Press in the Eighteenth Century* (1987), pp. 135–68; Harris, *London Newspapers in the Age of Walpole* (1987).
18. RA 55/67.
19. Stanhope to Sir Luke Schaub, 27 Ap. 1722, New York, Public Library, Hardwicke Collection vol. 59.
20. BL Add. 37388 f.201–2, 32686 f.152, 32689 f.127; Holmes, *The Electorate and the National Will in the First Age of Party* (Lancaster, 1976); N. Landau, 'Independence, Deference and Voter Participation: The Behaviour of the Electorate in Early Eighteenth-Century Kent', *Historical Journal*, 22 (1979), 561–84; J. C. D. Clark, *English Society*, pp. 15–26; W. A. Speck, 'The Electorate in the First Age of Party', in C. Jones (ed.) *Britain in the First Age of Party*, pp. 45–62; P. Langford, 'Property and "Virtual Representation" in Eighteenth-Century England', *Historical Journal*, 31 (1988), 83–115.
21. Surrey CRO Brodrick Mss 1248/7 f.23. N. Hunt, 'The Russian Company and the Government, 1730–42', *Oxford Slavonic Papers* 7(1957), 27–65; L. Sutherland, *The East India Company in Eighteenth-Century Politics* (Oxford, 1952).
22. Walpole to Townshend, 8 June 1723, PRO 43/66.
23. N. Rogers, 'Resistance to Oligarchy: The City Opposition to

Walpole and his Successors, 1725–47', in J. Stevenson (ed.), *London in the Age of Reform* (Oxford, 1977), pp. 1–29; Rogers, 'The City Elections Act (1725) reconsidered', *English Historical Review*, 100 (1985), 604–17.

24. L. Penson, 'The London West India Interest in the Eighteenth Century', *English Historical Review*, 36 (1921), 373–92; R. Sheridan, 'The Molasses Act and the Market Strategy of the British Sugar Planters', *Journal of Economic History*, 17 (1957), 62–83.

25. Black, 'Foreign Policy in the Age of Walpole' in Black (ed.), *Britain in the Age of Walpole*, pp. 158–9; Black, *Foreign Policy in the Age of Walpole*, pp. 93–117.

26. Woodfine, 'Anglo-Spanish War', pp. 185–209.

27. Hunt, *Two Early Political Associations: The Quakers and the Dissenting Deputies in the Age of Sir Robert Walpole* (Oxford, 1961).

28. N. Sykes, *Edmund Gibson, Bishop of London* (Oxford, 1926); Sykes, *Church and State in England in the Eighteenth Century* (Cambridge, 1934).

29. Langford, "Convocation and the Tory Clergy, 1717–61', in E. Cruickshanks and Black (eds), *The Jacobite Challenge* (Edinburgh, 1988), pp. 107–22.

30. J. D. Walsh, 'Origins of the Evangelical Revival', in Bennett and Walsh (eds), *Essays in Modern Church History* (1966); F. Baker, *John Wesley and the Church of England* (1970).

31. B. R. Kreiser, *Miracles, Convulsions and Ecclesiastical Politics in Early Eighteenth-Century Paris* (Princeton, 1978).

32. Hunt, *Political Associations*, p. 159.

33. *A Letter on a Proposed Alteration of the 39 Articles by Lord Walpole written 1751* (1863), pp. 5–6.

34. Cobbett, XIII, 272, 562, 564–5, 617.

35. R. Browning, *Political and Constitutional Ideas of the Court Whigs* (Baton Rouge, 1982).

36. J. McLachlan, *Trade and Peace with Old Spain, 1667–1750* (Cambridge, 1940).

37. NLS MS 7046 f.38; Carew to Sydenham *et al.*, 22 Ap. 1742, Taunton CRO Trollop–Bellew papers, DD/TB, box 16 OB8.

38. Earl of March, *A Duke and his Friends* (2 vols, London, 1911), I, p. 165; Black, 'The Medal as Political Propaganda', *Medal*, 10 (1986), 8–10; NLS MS 7045 f.92.

39. P. Borsay, 'The English Urban Renaissance: the Development of Provincial Urban Culture *c*1680–*c*1760', *Social History*, 5 (1977), 581–603; P. Corfield, *The Impact of English Towns 1700–1800* (Oxford, 1982); P. Clark (ed.), *The Transformation of English Towns 1600–1800* (1984); Borsay, *The English Urban Renaissance: Culture*

and Society in the Provincial Town 1660–1770 (Oxford, 1989).

40. BL Add. 47028 f.97.

41. BL Add. 32688 f.30; *Victoria County History. East Riding*, I (London, 1969), pp. 201–2; BL Add. 47000 f.116; *York Courant*, 20 Oct. 1741; L. Cust, *Records of the Cust Family Series*, III (1927), pp. 32–3.

42. Plumb, *The Commercialization of Leisure in Eighteenth-Century England* (Reading, 1973); J. McKendrick *et al.*, *The Birth of a Consumer Society* (1982).

43. Black, 'Grain Exports and Neutrality', *Journal of European Economic History*, 12 (1983), 593–600.

44. BL Add. 32688 f.257; 35406 f.140; *York Courant*, 27 Oct 1741.

45. A. Charlesworth (ed.), *An Atlas of Rural Protest in Britain 1548–1900* (1983); Cobbett, X, 249–50; NLS MS 7046 f.22; BL Add. 47028 f.91; E. Stockdale, *Law and Order in Georgian Bedfordshire* (Bedford, 1982), p. 11.

46. PRO 30/29/1/11 f.276.

47. HMC *Egmont* I, 220.

48. PRO 105/282 f.347.

49. Coxe, *Memoirs . . . Orford*, I, 264–5, II, 340; Sedgwick (ed.), Hervey, *Materials*, I, 135–43; H. T. Dickinson, *Bolingbroke* (1970), p. 219.

50. Dickinson, 'Popular Politics in the Age of Walpole', in Black (ed.), *Britain in the Age of Walpole* (1984), p. 68.

51. PRO 78/290 f.78; BL Add. 34465, 32782, Liston to the Foreign Secretary, the Marquis of Carmarthen, 16 Ap. (ns) 1787, Waldegrave, envoy in Paris, to Newcastle, 14 Oct. (ns) 1733.

52. Anon., *The Last Will and Testament of the Right Hon. Robert Earl of Orford* (London, 1745).

53. G. H. Jones, *The Mainstream of Jacobitism* (Cambridge, Mass., 1954); Black, 'Jacobitism and British Foreign Policy under the First Two Georges', *Royal Stuart Papers*, 32 (1988); Black, 'Jacobitism and British Foreign Policy' in E. Cruickshanks and Black (eds), *The Jacobite Challenge* (Edinburgh, 1988), pp. 142–60; Black, *Culloden and the '45* (Gloucester, 1990).

54. *Northampton Mercury*, 28 Oct. 1723.

55. Earl Stanhope (ed.), *Miscellanies* (1863), pp. 67–9.

4 PARTY AND POLITICS UNDER THE FIRST TWO GEORGES

1. P. Thomas, 'Party Politics in Eighteenth-Century Britain', *British Journal for Eighteenth-Century Studies*, 10 (1987), 205. I have benefited greatly from discussing this article with Stephen Baskerville.

2. Sedgwick (ed.), *House of Commons*, I, p. 377; HL STG Box 22 (9); Lonsdale to Fleming, 30 Oct. 1737, 20 Sept. 1740, Carlisle, D/Sen/Fleming 14.

3. Reading, Berkshire Record Office, D/E Hy 04; Interesting works include G. Bage, 'A Provincial Reaction to the French Revolution: radical politics, social unrest and the growth of loyal opinion in East Anglia at the end of the eighteenth century, with special reference to the county of Suffolk' (Cambridge, MLitt, 1983); S. Baskerville, 'The Management of the Tory Interest in Lancashire and Cheshire, 1714–47' (Oxford, DPhil, 1976); A. Newman, 'Elections in Kent and its Parliamentary Representation 1715–54' (Oxford, DPhil, 1957); J. F. Quinn, 'Political Activity in Yorkshire *c*.1700–1742' (University of Lancaster, MLitt, 1980); D. O'Sullivan, 'Politics in Norwich, 1701–1835' (University of East Anglia, MPhil, 1975); K. von den Steinen, 'The Fabric of an Interest: the First Duke of Dorset and Kentish and Sussex Politics, 1705–65' (University of California, Los Angeles, PhD, 1969); P. Jenkins, *The Making of a Ruling Class: The Glamorgan Gentry 1640–1790* (Cambridge, 1983); J. Triffitt, 'Politics and the Urban Community: Parliamentary Boroughs in the South West of England, 1710–1730' (Oxford, DPhil, 1985).

4. L. Glassey, 'Local Government', in Jones (ed.), *Britain in the First Age of Party*, p. 171; Lowther to John Spedding, 25 Aug. 1743, Carlisle, Cumbria RO D/Lons/W2/1/104.

5. J. M. Black, 'Eighteenth-Century Electioneering: A Yorkshire Example', *Yorkshire Archaeological Journal*, 59 (1987), 191; Hertford, CRO D/EP F196 f.74; *Gazette d'Amsterdam*, 16 Nov. (ns) 1725.

6. G. Holmes (ed.), *Britain after the Glorious Revolution 1689–1714* (1969), p. 235; Thomas, 'Party Politics', p. 205.

7. Thomas, 'Sir Roger Newdigate's Essays on Party, *c*.1762', *English Historical Review*, 102 (1987), 394–400.

8. Anon., *A Second Letter to Dr. Codex* (1734), p. 12; *Daily Gazetteer*, 1 Sept. 1735; BL Add. 47021 B f.55; *Old England*, 16 Feb. 1745.

9. Robert Freebairne to Hay, 8 Jan. 1722, Earl of Orrery to the Pretender, 30 June 1727, RA 57/18, 107/150; James Craggs, Whig MP, to the Earl of Stair, 6 Dec. 1716, SRO, GD 135/147

No. 10; Broglie, French envoy, to Morville, French foreign minister, 30 Nov. (ns) 1724, Chammorel, French *chargé d'affaires*, to Morville, 12 Feb. (ns) 1725, AE.CP.Ang. 349 f.299, 350f.134; Ossorio, Sardinian envoy in London, to Charles Emmanuel III, 7 Jan. (ns) 1735, Turin, Archivio di Stato, Lettere Ministri Inghilterra 42.

10. Thomas, 'Party Politics', p. 204; BL Add. 23825 f.276–7.

11. Newcastle to Townshend, 18 Aug. 1722, Beinecke, Osborn Files, Newcastle; BL Add. 32686 f.236.

12. BL Add. 37366 f.95. 47028 f.207, Stowe 232 f.51; Colley, *Defiance*, pp. 192–3; Duke of Chandos to Harcourt, 3 Nov. 1717, HL. ST 57 vol. 13, p. 79.

13. BL Add. 32686 f.330, Stowe 242 f.212; RA 26/32; HL ST. 57 vol. 13, p. 92.

14. Bodl. Add. Ms A.269, pp. 74–5.

15. BL Add. 32686 f.269.

16. Colley, *Defiance*, pp. 174, 50.

17. Browning review of Colley, *Albion*, 14 (1982), 311–12; Colley, *Defiance*, p. 55.

18. Black review of Colley, *British Journal for Eighteenth Century Studies*, 6 (1983), 96–8; Gibbs, 'English Attitudes towards Hanover and the Hanoverian Succession in the First Half of the Eighteenth Century', in A. M. Birke and K. Kluxen (eds), *England and Hanover* (Munich, 1986), p. 49.

19. Colley, *Defiance*, p. 208; Black, *The Collapse of the Anglo-French Alliance 1727–1731* (Gloucester, 1987), p. 19.

20. E. Gregg, *The Protestant Succession in International Politics 1710–1716* (New York, 1986), p. 297.

21. Baugh review of Hatton, *Journal of Modern History*, 53 (1981), 107.

22. Christie, 'The Tory Party, Jacobitism and the Forty-Five: A Note', *Historical Journal*, 30 (1987), 931.

23. D. McKay, 'Bolingbroke, Oxford and the Defence of the Utrecht Settlement in Southern Europe', *English Historical Review*, 86 (1971), 264–84; Toland, *State Anatomy* (3rd edn, 1917), pp. 17, 25; Coxe, *Memoirs . . . Orford*, II, p. 128; HL LO 7948.

24. P. Langford, *The Excise Crisis* (Oxford, 1975).

25. Black, 'England's "Ancien Régime"', *History Today*, 38 (March, 1988), 47–9.

26. Hayton, 'The "Country" interest and the party system, 1689–*c*.1720' in C. Jones (ed.), *Party and Management in Parliament, 1660–1784* (Leicester, 1984), pp. 65–6.

27. Clark, *The Dynamics of Change. The Crisis of the 1750s and English*

Party Systems (Cambridge, 1982), p. 454; Clark, 'A General Theory of Party, Opposition and Government, 1688–1832', *Historical Journal*, 23 (1980), 302–6.

28. Christie, 'The Changing Face of Parliamentary Politics, 1742–1789', in Black (ed.), *British Politics and Society from Walpole to Pitt, 1742–1789* (London, 1990).

29. Clark, 'The Decline of Party, 1740–1760', *English Historical Review*, 93 (1978), 517–19; L. Namier, *England in the Age of the American Revolution* (2nd edn, London, 1963), pp. 192–5.

30. Important recent work includes S. Baxter, 'The Conduct of the Seven Years War' in Baxter (ed.), *England's Rise to Greatness*, pp. 323–48; Schweizer (ed.), *Bute*; P. D. Brown and Schweizer, *The Devonshire Diary* (1982), pp. 57, 25, 52.

31. Namier and J. Brooke (eds), *The History of Parliament. The House of Commons 1754–1790* (3 vols, 1964), II, p. 487.

32. Namier, 'Monarchs and the Party System', in *Crossroads of Power: Essays on England in the Eighteenth Century* (1962), pp. 213–34; I. R. Christie, *The End of North's Ministry 1780–1782* (1958), pp. 188–230; Christie, 'Party in Politics in the Age of Lord North's Administration', *Parliamentary History*, 6 (1987), 47–8, 62.

33. Christie, *Wilkes, Wyvill and Reform: The Parliamentary Reform Movement in British Politics 1760–1785* (1962); J. Brewer, *Party Ideology and Popular Politics at the Accession of George III* (Cambridge, 1976).

34. Mure to Elliot, 8 Feb. 1762, NLS Mss 11010 f.9; P. Thomas, *Lord North* (1976).

5 THE BRITISH DIMENSION

1. J. S. Gibson, *Playing the Scottish Card. The Franco-Jacobite Invasion of 1708* (Edinburgh, 1988).

2. HMC *Egmont* I, p. 220; RA 103/80.

3. BL Add. 51417 f.77; Elliot to his father, Lord Minto, 15 Nov. 1755, NLS Mss 11001 f.15.

4. BL Add. 47028 f.21.

5. Wodrow, *Analecta* (4 vols, Edinburgh, 1842–3), p. 280.

6. BL Add. 61494 f.4.

7. Delafaye to Townshend, 22 Oct. 1725, PRO 43/75.

8. P. Riley, *The English Ministers and Scotland 1707–1727* (1964); J. M. Simpson, 'Who Steered the Gravy Train, 1707–1766?' in N. T. Phillipson and R. Mitchison (eds), *Scotland in the Age of Improvement*

(1970), pp. 47–72; Riley, *The Union of England and Scotland* (Manchester, 1978); B. Lenman, *The Jacobite Risings in Britain 1689–1746* (1980); Mitchison, *Lordship to Patronage: Scotland, 1603–1745* (1933); J. S. Shaw, *The Management of Scottish Society, 1707–64* (Edinburgh, 1983); E. G. Wehrli, 'Scottish Politics in the Age of Walpole' (Chicago, PhD, 1983).

9. Poyntz to Weston, 24 Sept. 1745, Farmington Connecticut, Weston papers vol. 16.

10. PRO 43/6 f.244, 282.

11. PRO 35/57 f.250, 35/59 f.183.

12. G. Elliot, *The Border Elliots* (Edinburgh, 1897), pp. 309–10; PRO 54/19 f.117. See also f.111, 115, 135.

13. Wodrow, *Analecta*, III, p. 273; F. McLynn, *France and the Jacobite Rising of 1746* (Edinburgh, 1981).

14. H. Wickes, *Regiments of Foot* (Reading, 1974); BL Blakeney Mss vol. 1, p. 64.

15. Cobbett, XIII, 354.

16. Dalrymple to Gilbert Elliot, 26 Feb. 1763, NLS Mss 11016 f.56; *St. James's Chronicle* 17 Dec. 1771; A. Murdoch, *'The People Above'. Politics and Administration in Mid-Eighteenth-Century Scotland* (Edinburgh, 1980) p. 19.

17. PRO 63/393 f.14.

18. RA 94/54; AE.CP.Ang. 373 f.233.

19. PRO 35/59 f.182.

20. Craggs to Stanhope, 30 Oct. 1719, PRO 43/58.

21. Hertford, County Record Office, D/EP F56 f.33–6; B. Williams, *The Whig Supremacy 1715–1760* (2nd edn, Oxford, 1962), p. 295; D. Hayton, 'Walpole and Ireland', in Black (ed.), *Britain in the Age of Walpole* (1984), p. 97; T. W. Moody and W. E. Vaughan (eds), *Eighteenth-Century Ireland 1691–1800* (Oxford, 1986).

22. *A List of the Absentees of Ireland* (Dublin, 1729); *The Present State of Ireland Considered* (Dublin, 1730), pp. 7, 19; *Some Observations on the present State of Ireland, particularly in relation to the Woollen Manufacture* (London, 1971), p. 21.

23. *Some Observations*, p. 12; *Remarks on the English Woollen Manufactures* (1730).

24. Townshend to Walpole, 23 Aug. 1724, Beinecke, Osborn Files, Townshend; A. Goodwin, 'Wood's Halfpence', *English Historical Review*, 51 (1936), 647–74.

25. Hertford, CRO D/EP F56 f.17–19.

26. F. G. James, 'The Irish Lobby in the Early Eighteenth Century', *English Historical Review*, 71 (1966), 543–57.

27. BL Add. 32687 f.54.
28. Surrey CRO Brodrick Mss 1248/7 f.17–18.
29. Derby Library, Catton Collection WH 3430, p. 102, 3431, p. 523.

CONCLUSION

1. Beinecke, Osborn Shelves, Stair Letters, No. 3.
2. Lynch, *The Independent Patriot* (1737), p. 31.
3. Wodrow, *Analecta*, III, p. 156.
4. AE.CP.Ang. 376 f.91.
5. Cobbett, XI, 921, 1118.
6. HL MO 4557.

A NOTE ON SOURCES

One of the best approaches to a study of early eighteenth-century Britain is a reading of some of the many sources of the period that survive. There are guides to and extracts from some of the sources of the period. Particularly important are D. B. Horn and M. Ransome (eds), *English Historical Documents, 1714–1783* (London, 1957); L. W. Hanson (ed.), *Contemporary Printed Sources for British and Irish Economic History, 1701–1750* (Cambridge, 1963); H. T. Dickinson (ed.), *Politics and Literature in the Eighteenth Century* (London, 1974); and S. Copley (ed.), *Literature and the Social Order in Eighteenth-Century England* (London, 1984). Many of the newspapers from the period can be read in the reference or local studies departments of major public libraries. There are important accessible collections in many towns, including Bristol, Bury St Edmunds, Canterbury, Chester, Derby, Exeter, Gloucester, Ipswich, Leeds, Newcastle, Northampton, Norwich, Nottingham and Reading.

Useful for the study of these newspapers are G. A. Cranfield, *The Development of the Provincial Newspaper, 1700–1760* (Oxford, 1962) and R. M. Wiles, *Freshest Advices* (Columbus, Ohio, 1965). Modern editions of extracts from newspapers include W. B. Coley (ed.), *The Jacobites Journal* (Oxford, 1982), and S. Varey (ed.), *Lord Bolingbroke: Contributions to the Craftsman* (Oxford, 1982). Excellent modern editions of Defoe, Fielding, Gay, Johnson, Pope and Swift have made the literature of the period readily accessible.

Much political material from the period is in print. Particularly useful are W. Coxe, *Memoirs of the Life and Administration of Sir Robert Walpole, Earl of Orford* (London, 1798), Lord Chancellor King's Notes in appendix to P. King, *Life of John Locke* (London, 1830), G. H. Rose, *A Selection from the Papers of the Earls of Marchmont* (London, 1831),

J. Graham, *Annals and Correspondence of the Viscount and the First and Second Earls of Stair* (Edinburgh, 1875), P. Yorke, *The Life and Correspondence of Philip Yorke, Earl of Hardwicke* (London, 1913), R. Sedgwick (ed.), *Some Materials towards Memoirs of the Reign of George II by John Lord Hervey* (London, 1931), T. J. McCann (ed.), *The Correspondence of the Dukes of Richmond and Newcastle 1724–50* (Lewes, 1984). Other useful collections are B. Dobrée (ed.), *The Letters of Philip Dormer Stanhope, Fourth Earl of Chesterfield* (London, 1932), M. Percival, *Political Ballads Illustrating the Administration of Sir Robert Walpole* (Oxford, 1916), and D. Warren (ed.), *More Culloden papers* 3 (Inverness, 1927). The volumes of *British Diplomatic Instructions* in the Camden third series are very useful for foreign policy. Many volumes of the Historical Manuscripts Commission reports are of great importance. Particularly noteworthy are the Carlisle, Onslow, Polwarth, Portland, Stuart, Townshend, Trevor and Weston papers and the Egmont Diary.

SELECT BIBLIOGRAPHY

This list has had to be restricted for reasons of space. Many works cited in the References have not been cited again. Unless otherwise noted, the place of publication for all books is London.

For comprehensive listings of recent works the reader should consult the Royal Historical Society's annual *Bibliography of British and Irish History*.

F. Baker, *John Wesley and the Church of England* (1970).

T. Bartlett and D. Hayton (eds), *Penal Era and Golden Age: Essays in Irish History, 1690–1800* (Belfast, 1979).

S. Baskerville (ed.), *Walpole in Power* (Oxford, 1985).

D. Baugh, *British Naval Administration in the Age of Walpole* (Princeton, 1965).

J. Beckett, 'A Back-Bench MP in the Eighteenth Century', *Parliamentary History*, 1 (1982), 79–97.

J. Beckett, *The Aristocracy of England, 1660–1914* (Oxford, 1986).

G. Bennett, 'Jacobitism and the Rise of Walpole', in N. McKendrick (ed.), *Historical Perspectives: Studies in English Thought and Society in honour of J. H. Plumb* (1974), pp. 70–92.

G. Bennett, *The Tory Crisis in Church and State 1688–1730: The Career of Francis Atterbury, Bishop of Rochester* (Oxford, 1975).

J. Black, '1733 – Failure of British Diplomacy?', *Durham University Journal*, 74 (1982), 199–209.

J. Black, 'George II Reconsidered', *Mitteilungen des Österreichischen Staatsarchivs*, 35 (1982), 35–56.

J. Black, 'An "Ignoramus" in European Affairs?', *British Journal for Eighteenth-Century Studies*, 6 (1983), 55–65.

J. Black, 'Parliament and the Political and Diplomatic Crisis of 1717–18', *Parliamentary History*, 3 (1984), 77–101.

J. Black (ed.), *Britain in the Age of Walpole* (1984).

J. Black, 'Press and Politics in the Age of Walpole', *Durham University Journal*, 77 (1984), 87–93.

J. Black, *British Foreign Policy in the Age of Walpole* (Edinburgh, 1985).

J. Black, *Natural and Necessary Enemies. Anglo-French Relations in the Eighteenth Century* (1986).

J. Black, 'Whig Popular Propaganda in the Early Eighteenth Century', *York Historian*, 7 (1986), 40–5.

J. Black, 'British Foreign Policy and the War of the Austrian Succession', *Canadian Journal of History*, 21 (1986), 313–31.

J. Black, 'Fresh Light on the Fall of Townshend', *Historical Journal*, 29 (1986), 41–64.

J. Black, *The English Press in the Eighteenth Century* (1987).

J. Black and P. Woodfine (eds), *The British Navy and the Use of Naval Power in the Eighteenth Century* (Leicester, 1988).

J. Black and K. Schweizer (eds), *Politics and the Press in Hanoverian Britain* (Lewiston, 1989).

J. Black, 'Britain's Foreign Alliances in the Eighteenth Century', *Albion*, 20 (1988), 573–602.

J. Black, 'The British State and Foreign Policy in the Eighteenth Century', *Trivium*, 23 (1988), 127–48.

J. Black, 'Jacobitism and British Foreign Policy under the First Two Georges', *Royal Stuart Papers*, 32 (1988).

J. Black (ed.), *Knights Errant and True Englishmen. British Foreign Policy 1660–1800* (Edinburgh, 1989).

J. Black, 'Additional Light on the Fall of Townshend', *Yale University Library Gazette* (1989), 132–6.

J. Black, 'In search of a scandalous pamphlet: Sir Robert Walpole and the attempt to suppress the publication of Opposition Literature in the United Provinces', *Publishing History*, 25 (1989), 5–11.

J. Black, 'Anglo-Austrian relations, 1725–1740. A Study in Failure', *British Journal for Eighteenth-Century Studies*, 12 (1989), 29–45.

J. Black, *The Rise of the European Great Powers 1679–1793* (1990).

J. Black, *Eighteenth Century Europe, 1700–89* (1990).

P. Borsay, 'The English Urban Renaissance: the Development of Provincial Urban Culture c.1680–c.1760', *Social History*, 5 (1977), 581–603.

J. Brewer and J. Styles (eds), *An Ungovernable People: The English and their Law in the Seventeenth and Eighteenth Centuries* (1980).

J. Brewer, *The Sinews of Power. War, Money and the English State, 1688–1783* (1989).

J. Broad, 'Whigs and Deer-Stealers in other Guises', *Past and Present*, 119 (May 1988).

R. Browning, *The Duke of Newcastle* (New Haven, Conn., 1975).

R. Browning, *Political and Constitutional Ideas of the Court Whigs* (Baton Rouge, Louisiana, 1982).

J. Cannon (ed.), *The Whig Ascendancy* (1981).

J. Cannon, *Aristocratic Century: The Peerage of Eighteenth-Century England* (Cambridge, 1984).

J. Clark, 'A General Theory of Party, Opposition and Government, 1688–1832', *Historical Journal*, 23 (1980), 295–325.

J. Clark, *The Dynamics of Change: The Crisis of the 1750s and English Party Systems* (Cambridge, 1982).

J. Clark, *English Society 1688–1832* (Cambridge, 1985).

J. Clark, *Revolution and Rebellion. State and Society in England in the Seventeenth and Eighteenth Centuries* (Cambridge, 1986).

J. Clark, 'English History's Forgotten Context: Scotland, Ireland, Wales', *Historical Journal*, 32 (1989), 211–28.

P. Clark (ed.), *The Transformation of English Towns 1600–1800* (1984).

P. Clark, 'The "Mother Gin" controversy in the early eighteenth century', *Transactions of the Royal Historical Society*, 5th ser. 31 (1981), 1–19.

L. Colley, 'Eighteenth-Century English Radicalism before Wilkes', *Transactions of the Royal Historical Society*, 5th ser. 31 (1981), 1–19.

L. Colley, *In Defiance of Oligarchy: The Tory Party 1714–60* (Cambridge, 1982).

P. Corfield, *The Impact of English Towns 1700–1800* (Oxford, 1982).

W. Coxe, *Memoirs of the Life and Administration of Sir Robert Walpole, Earl of Orford* (1798).

E. Cruickshanks, *Political Untouchables: The Tories and the '45* (1979).

E. Cruickshanks, *Ideology and Conspiracy: Aspects of Jacobitism, 1689–1759* (Edinburgh, 1982).

E. Cruickshanks and J. Black (eds), *The Jacobite Challenge* (Edinburgh, 1988).

H. T. Dickinson, *Bolingbroke* (1970).

H. T. Dickinson, *Walpole and the Whig Supremacy* (1973).

H. T. Dickinson, *Liberty and Property: Political Ideology in Eighteenth-Century Britain* (1977).

H. T. Dickinson, 'Popular Politics in the Age of Walpole', in J. Black (ed.), *Britain in the Age of Walpole* (1984), pp. 45–68.

P. G. M. Dickson, *The Financial Revolution in England* (1967).

I. Doolittle, 'The City Elections Act', *English Historical Review*, 97 (1982), 504–29.

I. Doolittle, 'A first-hand account of the Commons debate on the removal of Sir Robert Walpole, 13 February 1741', *Bulletin of the Institute of Historical Research*, 53 (1982), 125–40.

A. Downie, *Robert Harley and the Press* (Cambridge, 1979).

A. Foord, *His Majesty's Opposition* (Oxford, 1964).

P. Fritz, *The English Ministers and Jacobitism* (Toronto, 1975).

B. Goldgar, *Walpole and the Wits* (Lincoln, Nebraska, 1976).

E. Gregg, *Queen Anne* (1980).

M. Harris, 'Print and Politics in the Age of Walpole', in J. Black (ed.), *Britain in the Age of Walpole* (1984), pp. 189–210.

M. Harris, *London Newspapers in the Age of Walpole* (1987).

R. Hatton, *George I* (1978).

W. J. Hausman and J. L. Neufeld, 'Excise Anatomised: The Political Economy of Walpole's 1733 Tax Scheme', *Journal of European Economic History*, 10 (1981), 131–43.

D. Hay, P. Linebaugh and E. P. Thompson, *Albion's Fatal Tree: Crime and Society in Eighteenth-Century England* (1975).

T. Herbert and G. E. Jones (eds), *The Remaking of Wales in the Eighteenth Century* (Cardiff, 1988).

B. W. Hill, *The Growth of Parliamentary Parties 1689–1742* (1976).

B. W. Hill, *British Parliamentary Parties, 1742–1832* (1985).

B. W. Hill, *Sir Robert Walpole* (1989).

G. Holmes, 'Sir Robert Walpole', in H. van Thal (ed.), *The Prime Ministers* (2 vols, 1974).

G. Holmes, 'The achievement of stability: the social context of politics from the 1680s to the age of Walpole', in J. Cannon (ed.), *The Whig Ascendancy* (1981), pp. 1–22.

G. Holmes, *Augustan England: Professions, State and Society 1680–1730* (1982).

G. Holmes, 'Eighteenth-Century Toryism', *Historical Journal*, 26 (1983), 755–60.

G. Holmes, *Politics, Religion and Society in England, 1679–1742* (1986).

T. Horne, 'Politics in a Corrupt Society: William Arnall's Defence of Robert Walpole', *Journal of the History of Ideas*, 41 (1980).

N. Hunt, 'The Russia Company and the Government, 1730–42', *Oxford Slavonic Papers*, 7 (1957), 27–65.

N. Hunt, *Two Early Political Associations* (Oxford, 1961).

P. Jenkins, *The Making of a Ruling Class: The Glamorgan Gentry, 1640–1790* (Cambridge, 1983).

C. Jones (ed.), *British in the First Age of Party 1680–1750* (1987).

C. Jones (ed.), *A Pillar of the Constitution: The House of Lords in British Politics, 1603–1784* (1989).

G. Jones, *The Mainstream of Jacobitism* (Cambridge, Mass., 1954).

B. Kemp, *Sir Robert Walpole* (1976).

T. Kendrick, 'Sir Robert Walpole, the Old Whigs and the Bishops, 1733–1736: a Study in Eighteenth-Century Parliamentary Politics', *Historical Journal*, 11 (1968), 421–45.

J. P. Kenyon, *Revolution Principles: The Politics of Party 1689–1720* (Cambridge, 1977).

I. Kramnick, *Bolingbroke and His Circle* (Cambridge, Mass., 1968).

N. Landau, *The Justices of the Peace 1679–1760* (Berkeley, Cal., 1984).

J. Langbein, 'Albion's Fatal Flaws', *Past and Present*, 98 (1983), 96–120.

P. Langford, *The Excise Crisis* (Oxford, 1975).

P. Langford, *A Polite and Commercial People. England 1727–1783* (Oxford, 1989).

B. Lenman, *The Jacobite Risings in Britain 1689–1746* (1980).

J. McKendrick *et al.*, *The Birth of a Consumer Society* (1982).

R. Malcolmson, *Life and Labour in England 1700–1780* (1981).

G. Midgley, *The Life of Orator Henley* (Oxford, 1973).

G. Mingay, *The Gentry: the Rise and Fall of a Ruling Class* (1976).

R. Mitchison, *Lordship to Patronage. Scotland 1603–1745* (1983).

A. Murdoch, *'The People Above', Politics and Administration in Mid-Eighteenth-Century Scotland* (Edinburgh, 1980).

A. Newman, *The Parliamentary Diary of Sir Edward Knatchbull 1722–30* (1963).

J. Owen, 'George II Reconsidered', in J. S. Bromley, P. Dickson and A. Whiteman (eds), *Statesmen, Scholars and Merchants* (Oxford, 1972), pp. 113–34.

R. Paulson, *Hogarth: His Life, Art and Times* (New Haven, Conn., 1971).

L. Penson, 'The London West India Interest in the Eighteenth Century', *English Historical Review*, 36 (1921), 373–92.

J. Plumb, *Sir Robert Walpole. The Making of a Statesman* (1956).

J. Plumb, *Sir Robert Walpole. The King's Minister* (1960).

J. Plumb, *Men and Places* (1963).

J. Plumb, *The Growth of Political Stability in England, 1675–1725* (1967).

J. Plumb, *The Commercialization of Leisure in Eighteenth-Century England* (Reading, 1973).

R. Porter, *English Society in the Eighteenth Century* (1982).

J. Price, 'The Excise Affair Revisited', in S. Baxter (ed.), *England's Rise to Greatness* (Berkeley, Cal., 1983).

J. F. Quinn, 'Yorkshiremen go to the Polls. County contests in the early eighteenth century', *Northern History*, 21 (1985), 137–74.

D. Reading, *The Anglo-Russian Commercial Treaty of 1734* (New Haven, Conn., 1938).

C. Realey, *The Early Opposition to Sir Robert Walpole* (Philadelphia, 1931).

J. Redwood, *Reason, Ridicule and Religion: The Age of Enlightenment in England 1660–1750* (1976).

C. Robbins, *The Eighteenth-Century Commonwealthman* (Cambridge, Mass., 1959).

C. Roberts, 'Party and Patronage in Later Stuart England', in S. Baxter (ed.), *England's Rise to Greatness* (Berkeley, Cal., 1983), pp. 185–212.

N. Rogers, 'Money, Land and Lineage: the Big Bourgeoisie of Hanoverian London', *Social History*, 4 (1979), 437–54.

N. Rogers, 'The Urban Opposition to Whig Oligarchy, 1720–60', in M. and J. Jacob (eds), *The Origins of Anglo-American Radicalism* (1984).

N. Rogers, 'The City Elections Act (1725) reconsidered', *English Historical Review*, 100 (1985), 604–17.

P. Rogers, 'The Waltham Blacks and the Black Act', *Historical Journal*, 17 (1974), 465–86.

R. Sedgwick, *The House of Commons 1715–54* (2 vols, 1970).

R. Sheridan, 'The Molasses Act and the Market Strategy of the British Sugar Planters', *Journal of Economic History*, 17 (1957), 62–83.

J. Simpson, 'Who steered the Gravy Train, 1707–1766?', in N. T. Phillipson and R. Mitchison (eds), *Scotland in the Age of Improvement* (Edinburgh, 1970).

Q. Skinner, 'The Principles and Practice of Opposition: the case of Bolingbroke versus Walpole', in N. McKendrick (ed.), *Historical Perspectives: Studies in English Thought and Society in honour of J. H. Plumb* (1974), pp. 93–128.

W. Speck, *Stability and Strife. England 1714–1760* (1977).

W. Speck, 'Whigs and Tories dim their glories: English political parties under the first two Georges', in J. Cannon (ed.), *The Whig Ascendancy* (1981), pp. 57–70.

W. Speck, *The Butcher. The Duke of Cumberland and the Suppression of the '45* (1981).

W. Speck, *Society and Literature in England, 1700–60* (Dublin, 1983).

J. Stevenson, *Popular Disturbances in England 1700–1870* (1979).

R. M. Sunter, *Patronage and Politics in Scotland, 1707–1832* (Edinburgh, 1986).

L. Sutherland, *The East India Company in Eighteenth-Century Politics* (Oxford, 1952).

L. Sutherland, 'The City of London in Eighteenth-Century Politics', in R. Pares and A. J. P. Taylor (eds), *Essays presented to Sir Lewis Namier* (1956), pp. 49–74.

L. Sutherland and L. G. Mitchell (eds), *The History of Oxford University. Volume V. The Eighteenth Century* (Oxford, 1986).

N. Sykes, *Edmund Gibson, Bishop of London* (Oxford, 1926).

N. Sykes, *Church and State in England in the Eighteenth Century* (Cambridge, 1934).

N. Sykes, *William Wake, Archbishop of Canterbury* (Cambridge, 1957).

S. Taylor, 'Church and Society after the Glorious Revolution', *Historical Journal*, 31 (1988), 973–87.

S. Taylor, 'British Politics in the Age of Holmes', *Parliamentary History*, 8 (1989), 132–41.

P. D. G. Thomas, 'Party Politics in Eighteenth-Century Britain: some Myths and a Touch of Reality', *British Journal for Eighteenth-Century Studies*, 10 (1987), 201–10.

E. P. Thompson, 'The Moral Economy of the English Crowd in the Eighteenth Century', *Past and Present*, 50 (1971).

E. P. Thompson, *Whigs and Hunters: The Origins of the Black Act* (1975).

M. Thomson, *The Secretaries of State, 1681–1782* (Oxford, 1932).

P. Vaucher, *Robert Walpole et la politique de Fleury* (Paris, 1924).

J. Walsh, 'Origins of the Evangelical Revival', in G. Bennett and J. Walsh (eds), *Essays in Modern Church History in Memory of Norman Sykes* (1966).

W. Ward, *The English Land Tax in the Eighteenth Century* (Oxford, 1953).

C. Wilson, *England's Apprenticeship, 1603–1763* (1965).

K. Wilson, 'Empire, Trade and Popular Politics in mid-Hanoverian Britain: the case of Admiral Vernon', *Past and Present*, 121 (1988), 74–109.

G. A. Wrigley and R. S. Schofield, *The Population of England, 1541–1871: A Reconstruction* (1981).

P. Yorke, 2nd Earl of Hardwicke, *Walpoliana* (1781).

INDEX

DATE DUE

HIGHSMITH 45-220